CRUCIFYING RELIGION

CRUCIFYING RELIGION

HOW JESUS IS THE END OF RELIGION

DONAVON RILEY

Crucifying Religion

© 2019 Donavon Riley

Published by:
1517 Publishing
PO Box 54032
Irvine, CA 92619–4032

Publisher's Cataloging-In-Publication Data
(Prepared by The Donohue Group, Inc.)

Names: Riley, Donavon, author.
Title: Crucifying religion : how Jesus is the end of religion / by Donavon Riley.
Description: Irvine, CA : 1517 Publishing, [2019] |
    Includes bibliographical references.
Identifiers: ISBN 9781948969246 (softcover) | ISBN 9781948969253 (ebook)
Subjects: LCSH: Jesus Christ—Teachings. | Bible. Gospels—Criticism,
    interpretation, etc. | Christian life—Biblical teaching. | Riley, Donavon—
    Religion. | Atonement.
Classification: LCC BT304.9 .R55 2019 (print) | LCC BT304.9 (ebook) |
    DDC 232—dc23

Printed in the United States of America

Cover art by Brenton Clarke Little

CONTENTS

CHAPTER 1

INTRODUCTION

My life can be summed up as an exodus from religion to Jesus Christ. I did not start out looking for God, or Jesus. I never wanted to walk into a place of worship, because it was of no value to me. The holy scriptures of different religions appealed to me only as anthologies of fantastic, mythical tales. Then, when I was twenty-three, a zealous atheist strung out on alcohol and drugs, and suicidal, my life was turned upside down. I came to believe there is a God, and worse yet (at that time, it was definitely a "worse yet") that this God had taken a personal interest in my path towards self-destruction. To get some perspective on what was happening, I read holy book after holy book. I talked with people who were religious. I had to know more about what people believed.

When it was clear God was not going to leave me alone, I decided to find a religion with the hope that it would relieve some or all of my anxiety and fear. I followed the teachings of the Qur'an. I studied the Tao Te Ching. I engaged in folk-religious rituals, new-age spiritual practices, and Tantric Buddhism. But none of these pursuits comforted my troubled conscience. It had the opposite effect. It seemed that the more I did to get God off my back by finding a religion or spiritual practice God could sign-off on, the more frustrated I became. The more I did, the more I felt God forcing his way into my life and choices, and not in a way that offered relief.

I pushed friends away. I drank more and used harder drugs in the hope that I would overdose. I stopped going out except to work so I could afford even more alcohol and drugs. Then, in desperation, I purchased a Bible. It was not an easy decision since I had a particular prejudice towards Christians. I thought they were juvenile and ignorant of reality. Yet, as I read the Bible, the more I learned about Jesus. He was no intangible, untouchable God. He was a God who became a man, loved sinners, and came to serve. This was very different from all that I had read and been taught about God and religion in the past. The Bible claimed I did not have to (because I couldn't) save myself. I didn't have to do anything to get God off my back. Instead, God came for me, gave himself as a gift to me, and asked for nothing in return. That was when I took my first tentative steps toward becoming a Christian, but instead of finding and joining a religion I found something entirely different.

What I found is that Jesus is the end of religion. All of them (save those of that faithful remnant that looked forward to his arrival) were redundant to begin with, but he makes plain the futility of them all. He did not show up to tweak Judaism or create a new self-salvation project or religion. When the nails were driven into his hands and feet, the spear pierced his side, and he said, "It is finished," all the religions and all the ways we imagine we can save ourselves by our sacrifices and offerings were crucified. In the silence of the tomb and resurrection thereafter, the question, "What must I do to be saved," received its answer. All the religions and their required sacrifices were rendered null and void by Jesus' once-and-for-all sacrifice.

Jesus' death and resurrection saves us from our religiosity, too. There are two passages from scripture that help illustrate what I mean. First, in John's gospel, when Jesus talked with the Samaritan woman,

The woman said to him, "Sir, I perceive that you are a prophet. Our fathers worshiped on this mountain, but you say that in Jerusalem is

the place where people ought to worship." Jesus said to her, "Woman,
believe me, the hour is coming when neither on this mountain nor in
Jerusalem will you worship the Father. You worship what you do not
know; we worship what we know, for salvation is from the Jews. But
the hour is coming, and is now here, when the true worshipers will
worship the Father in spirit and truth, for the Father is seeking such
people to worship him" (John 4:19-23).

She asked Jesus about religion and Israel's worship (which, by the
way, did not include her since she was both a Samaritan and a
woman of questionable moral character). But instead of pointing
her to Jerusalem, to the temple, the priests, and her sacrifices, he
said something unexpected. Jesus told her something she had
never heard before. Instead of telling her what she must do to be
saved, Jesus took everything she thought she knew about God,
worship, and living in a way that pleases God and turned it on
its head. He clarified the true worship of God for her. He pointed
her to worship in Spirit and truth. He pointed her to himself.
He pointed her to the living water that only he could provide.
In effect, Jesus told her that he was her oasis in the midst of a
religious wasteland.

Nowhere in the New Testament is Jesus' work for the Samaritan
woman, and for all of us, presented as just another spin on old-
time religion. Why? Religion is what we invent to bridge the
unbridgeable expanse between ourselves and God. The "wall of
separation" between God and us, as the apostle Paul writes in
his letter to the Ephesian churches (Ephesians 2:14), has been
broken down by the bloody suffering and death of Jesus.

There is nothing that divides us from God because of Jesus.
He breaks down and obliterates anybody and anything that tries
to get in his way. He—and not religion—is the way, truth, and
life. So why do we insist on constructing a new religion around
his teachings, his works, or his sacrificial death? The reason is
because Jesus is offensive. He refuses to be domesticated by us. In
the gospels, he undercuts every attempt by the religious leaders,

the crowds, and his own disciples to turn his teachings into a religion. He refused to play by their spiritual and moral rules.

The second example of Jesus' overturning of religion is found in the many instances when religious leaders tried to expose him as a charlatan and religious fraud through legal wrangling, Jesus turned the questions back on them in such a way that they came away from the argument looking lawless. For example, in Matthew 22:24–36 when religious people asked Jesus a law question, he gave them a law answer. "Teacher, which commandment is the greatest in Moses's teachings?" Jesus responded, saying, "Love the Lord your God with all your heart, with all your soul, and with all your mind." This is the greatest and most important commandment. Using the opportunity, he responded with his own question: "What do you think about the Messiah? Whose son is he?" He asked a gospel question to get a gospel answer. The religious leaders said: "David's son." Jesus asked more gospel questions, but after just one question the religious leaders had had enough of gospel questions.

The religious leaders, like any religious person, preferred a law question. A law question begs for a law answer. Gospel questions do not beg for a law answer. All religious questions beg for law answers. "What must I do to be saved?" begs for a "You must do this" answer. Jesus question, "Whose son is the Messiah?" begs for a "God does this for you" answer.

When we have had enough of gospel questions, then we want law answers. But there is never a law answer to a gospel question. "How do I become a baptized child of God?" begs for a "This is what God's Word with water and the Spirit do for you" answer. "How do I find a new life and hope?" begs for a "This is the blood of Christ shed for you for the forgiveness of sin" answer. "How do I get right with God and enjoy freedom and peace?" begs for a "You're sent a preacher who declares forgiveness, life, and salvation to you in Jesus' name" answer.

If we want a law answer to a gospel question, we must get ready for hell. The law is not given so we can get a "You must do this" answer. The law is given so our trespasses are increased beyond all measure. The law is given so we are shut up and have no excuses when God's furious anger and judgment overtake us. The law is given so our need for a gospel answer is made clear to us. The purpose of the law is not to give us a "You must do this" answer. The law is given to drive us to a "God must do this for you" answer.

Jesus does not give a law answer to the religious leaders' question so he can go out and try to save himself from God's furious anger and judgment. Jesus gives a law answer so the religious leaders will be forced to admit that it is impossible to "Love the Lord your God with *all* your heart, with *all* your soul, and with *all* your mind." But they will not admit that it is impossible for them to love God with all of themselves. They have invested too much of themselves in their religiosity. They have made it personal. So, rather than repent of their religiosity they stop asking Jesus questions.

They know what Jesus says is true and impossible for them to do. But what they do not know—and do not want to know—is that God commands the impossible so we will stop trying to do the impossible and admit that only God can do it. That is why Jesus says, "What's impossible for you is possible for God" (Luke 18:27). And he does do it *all* for us. He baptizes us, gives us his body and blood in the Lord's Supper, and preaches gospel forgiveness to us. He gives us his faith and his love so that we are free from all worry about his furious anger and judgment. We are so free that we get to love the Lord our God with all our hearts, with all our souls, and with all our minds. And when that's done, we get to love our neighbors, too.

We are free from law questions and law answers. We are free from the demands and threats of the law. We are free from fear, insecurity, and worry. We are free because faith in Jesus sets us free. We are free because Jesus is the fulfillment of the law. We are free because "when the Son sets you free, you are free indeed" (John 8:36).

But we need our categories. We cling to them for meaning and identity. We believe they provide us with time and choice. The way we divide up people, things, and divinity into categories of right and wrong, strong and weak, successes and failures, wise and foolish, useful and useless, godly and godless functions as the mechanisms of control that allow us to dictate the way it's going to be. Our compulsive need to construct categories is a manifestation of our need to not only participate with God in bringing about our salvation but also to be God in God's place. This is why Jesus is so offensive to us.

Jesus replaces our search for meaning and identity with himself. His cross is the meaning of our lives and "baptized child of God" is our identity. He trespasses our time and choices by coming closer to us than our next breath. He treats all people equitably regardless of whether they are a Pharisee or a woman caught in adultery. Jesus does not care whether one is a child of Abraham or a dog Gentile, a tax collector or a teacher of Israel, a high priest or a Samaritan. All people are considered by our Savior as sheep who need a shepherd, or perhaps a better analogy (that Jesus himself uses) is that we are children in need of a Father who will lead, guide, and instruct us with his faithful, loving kindness.

This agitates us. We consider anything that tears away time and choice from us as diabolical, even (or especially) when God is the one doing it to us. And the way God does it to us through Jesus annoys us even more. This is why we like to turn every text about Jesus and his work for us into a text that is about us and our work for God. When Jesus says, "I stand at the door and knock" (Revelation 3:20), we poor sinners actually think we have the ability to open the door. When Jesus says, "Take up your cross and follow me" (Matthew 16:24), we think we can, even though Peter's example in the same text shows us that for all our well-meaning attempts to take up our cross, or any cross, to follow our Lord results in us trying to tear Jesus down off his cross. We see this often at the Lord's Table. Jesus says, "Unless you eat my flesh and drink my blood there is no life in you" (John 6:53), and we argue about what he means. What he means is, "Just eat the bread! It is my body, and, by the way, the wine is my blood given and shed for you for the forgiveness of your pious attempts to explain me away."

But that will not do for us. Jesus does not leave us any room to think, act, or get ourselves worked up to the proper level of religious fervor. How can we know whether God favors or condemns us when Jesus is claiming all the verbs of salvation for himself? For example, "I am the Way, the Truth, and the Life" (John 14:6). "I have come to seek and save the lost" (Luke 19:20). "No one comes to the Father except through me" (John 14:6), and so on. He seems so specific, so narrow, so particular in the way he wants to be preached, revealed, and worshiped by us.

Jesus is just too restrictive. He seems to want to strip us of everything we bring to the table that can assist him in working out our salvation—not just the worst parts either, but even our best attributes. Instead of, "This is the work of God, that you obey his commands," Jesus says, "This is the work of God, that you believe in him whom he has sent" (John 6:29). Instead of telling us to clean up our lives, go to church, and earn our salvation, the apostle says, "For by grace you have been saved through faith. And this is not your own doing; it is the gift of God" (Ephesians 2:8). Instead of pointing us to ourselves, to our thoughts and words and works, it is revealed to us that "in him we live and move and have our being" (Acts 17:28).

Jesus will not play by our rules. He refuses to scratch our religious itch. He does not give us the go-ahead to erect a religious scaffolding around him that we call "the Christian religion." This really annoys us because it is a pretty good religion as far as religions go. We focus a good amount of our attention on obedience to God's commandments. We make sure to exhort each other to come to church and put in our God time come Sunday as well as to live in such a way that God will look down upon us and reward us for our good works. Christianity is like the religion of the Jews, but better because we have free-trade coffee and we welcome everyone! And yet, for all our claims that this Christian religion is different and better than other religions, it is more of the same. We just use Jesus to make us look respectable in the marketplace of religions.

We do not preach a Jesus that is a stumbling block to religious types. He is not an offense to our moral sensibilities. In fact, we preach a Jesus who can offer something of value to everyone. But there is a trade-off. The gospel is not good news for sinners anymore. It is alright news that motivates us, more or less. And words like *grace, truth, faith, hope, forgiveness, blessing, salvation, redemption, sanctification,* and so on are ideas in search of meaning rather than words that are used synonymously for Jesus. Our churches have been captivated for so long by an addiction to spirituality and morality that we do not even recognize (or even care anymore) that the very people Jesus came to seek and save are the people we strive to keep out of our safe, predictable, comfortable communion.

Robert Farrar Capon once wrote, "Christianity is the proclamation of the end of religion, not of a new religion, or even the best of all possible religions. And therefore, if the cross is the sign of anything, it's the sign that God has gone out of the religion business and solved all the world's problems without requiring a single human being to do a single religious thing."[1] Now that Christendom is dead and we no longer have a voice in the public square, our socio-political and religious causes can no longer prop up the church. We have been exposed as a gospel-less, grace-less, Christ-less Christian religion. And the only way forward is to go back to the roots of our faith and confession. What is religion? If Jesus is the end of religion, then why do we construct a religion around him? And what are we supposed to do with so much free time if we are set free from the need to be religious? This book is my attempt to answer these questions.

---

[1] Robert Farrar Capon, *The Mystery of Christ* (Eerdmans, 1993), 62.

I am sure there are people who can do a much better job giving answers to these questions than me. But this is a book I need to write for myself as much as for you, brothers and sisters. In a way, this work is my confession. For twenty years, I have bounced from one church group to another in search of a place where I can enjoy fellowship. But with each group has come a set of criteria for how to believe, behave, and belong. And the more I have tried to adapt myself to the group, the more frustrated, depressed, and anxious I have become. It seems I was not wired to play by their rules. I have always been a button pusher, asking questions like: What does this have to do with Jesus? Did Jesus have to die for you to preach this? I thought the purpose and goal of his commands is love, not obedience and behavior modification?

It was a long time before I recognized that what I was pushing back against were attempts by each group to add their own religious spin to Christianity. What was offered to me as faithfulness was just original sin masquerading as piety. It was the old Adam's attempt to add his voice to God's Word. It was Christianity that had been transformed into a self-renovation project.

The reason I struggle (and have given up trying) to fit in, at least from where I am at today, is that I came into the church as an adult convert. An atheist turned believer, I was raised to loathe religion and all that comes with it. Growing up I was taught that Christians in particular are stupid, willfully ignorant people who hide from reality behind what they call God. This is why when I came to believe in a God through my reading of philosophy and science, and eventually theology, it was not an easy buy-in for me. Which religion is right? Which doctrines will help me understand God and my life's purpose? Should I worship in a synagogue, a mosque, an ashram, or a church? Does God even want me to worship him or her or it in a building? Is worship liturgical or spontaneous? Do I worship God in my imagination, by processing my emotions, or on top of Mount Hood? And what about all these checklists?

I did not really want to believe in a specific God. When I inter-acted with believers, they insisted I think, speak, and act a cer-tain way if I wanted their God to pay attention to me—the "right" kind of attention. But for someone who did not see the need for such specificity, the rules, rubrics, traditions, and jargon of these groups only offered me an excuse to avoid believers. I ran away from believers and churches and God, and yet here I am today, a Lutheran pastor. Even though I have given up trying to fit in, I am now as much a part of a religious system as anybody.

That is another reason why I am writing this book. It is why I need to write this book: my life is an exodus from religion to Christ Jesus. And if you are reading this, maybe it will help give form and meaning to what you have experienced, too. According to the Bible's teaching, the gospel reveals that Jesus takes our religiosity, hangs it on his cross, and sets us free through the faithfulness of God to be a child of our heavenly Father.

The gospel of Jesus Christ sets us free to worship him in Spirit and truth. He sets us free by joining his word with simple earthly things like water, bread, and wine, to trust that he does everything for us. The good news of Jesus Christ reveals that all of life is gift, even our afflictions. Jesus sets us free to love every-one we meet, even our most hated enemies, as one for whom he died. And every day as we recommit the original rebellion against God, when we take for ourselves what is not given to us in the way of gift, he comes and reclaims us as his own, cutting us loose from our need for the dope of religion. Jesus comes to crucify our religion, to set us free to live, love, and hope in him alone and announce this amazing good news to everyone we meet who is still crushed under the weight of religion.

CHAPTER 2

WHICH WAY TO GOD?

As a kid, I always wanted to believe there is a God, but I don't remember a time that I didn't question his very existence. Whether I was on my bed reading or crawling through the woods behind my best friend's house defending our town from Nazis, the Viet Cong, or Darth Vader and the forces of the Empire, my thoughts often wandered toward questions about belonging, safety, and questions that began with "why." Why was my dad always so angry? Why did I feel like I didn't fit in? Why, if there was a God, would he allow my cousin to die forty-five minutes after she was born? Suffering from abuse at home and bullying at school, wondering why Nazis were allowed to exist and babies die, I swung back and forth emotionally as a child between scared and angry. I was scared to go home, and when I was home I was scared to leave my room because I did not know which version of my dad waited to meet me. I was angry because I just wanted to fit in and be accepted. I was also angry because it did not seem like my peers were bothered by such questions, and when I did invite their feedback all I received was ridicule. I wanted to believe in God, but I could not reconcile what was happening all around me with the idea that there was something bigger than abuse, bullies, and death. I wanted to believe in God. I just couldn't.

That is how it went for me for years, oscillating between wanting to believe and rejecting belief. I was not raised in a religious household. My parents did not discuss God or religion unless it was to dismiss people's beliefs. My father, in particular, was violently opposed to any talk about God. He had lost his faith almost as soon as he touched ground in Vietnam in 1968. On his first day in country, the company he had been attached to since training camp was sent into the jungle to join up with other soldiers who were already engaged in a firefight. By the end of the day, my father was the only one out of a hundred men who survived the battle.

The only time he would talk about what happened to him during two tours of duty in Vietnam was when he was drunk or stoned. He would talk about a friend whose body was obliterated by a grenade before his very eyes. He would ramble on about malaria, rats the size of small dogs, and the horror of having to shoot women and children who ran at him with knives, pistols, or grenades. The young man, who once played piano at a Methodist church and dreamed of becoming an artist, could not reconcile his childhood beliefs with what he saw and experienced in Vietnam. Like Ivan in Dostoyevsky's great novel, *The Brothers Karamazov*, my father simply returned the ticket. Where was God when 99 young men had their lives cut short by lead and shrapnel? For my father, the answer was that there was no God. That is why those young men died.

My mother's unbelief was of a different sort. More agnostic than atheist, she left religion before puberty took hold. She grew up attending the Roman mass with her grandmother. But since the mass was spoken in Latin, and she did not understand the rituals and traditions of the Roman Church or have the courage to ask questions, she gave up on her grandmother's religion. She thought she did not belong in church. Everybody else seemed to know what to do and when to speak. The priest seemed unapproachable. The people seemed to come in and go out without much recognition of other worshipers. Church, for my mother, was a cold, impersonal, and strange place. The rituals and rites confused her. The words of the mass were unfathomable. So, she stopped going. And after my father returned from Vietnam, any doubts she may have harbored about her relation to God or church were squelched by his anger and addiction.

Growing up, we simply did not talk about God or religion. When mentioned, it evoked disgust from my father. He taught me that there was no God. Anyone who believe otherwise was a stupid, ignorant person who used religion as a crutch. This was especially true of Christians. Christians were naive people. They were two-faced, judgmental types. We avoided Christians as much as possible, except the ones that lived next door who hired me to babysit. Their money was good; we just didn't want to hear anything about their beliefs. When they invited us to church, we turned down the offer. In this way, my parents kept me insulated from God and his followers.

When I was eight or nine my aunt and uncle, who had recently left a cult, gave me a *Children's Illustrated Bible* for Christmas. They were concerned, they said, that I was growing up without any kind of relationship with God. My mother offered them a fake smile and thanked them for the gift. My father grumbled something but left the gift alone. This was my first exposure, that I remember, to a religious book. Its pictures fueled my imagination. However, they also seemed to me to be older versions of the same stories I read about in my favorite comic books. For example, The strength and bravery of Samson and David seemed similar, in my imagination, to stories about Thor and Captain America. But the illustrations did get me thinking about the whole matter of God. What kind of God got mad and drowned people and gave a man the strength to kill a lion and another the ability to survive three days in the belly of a giant fish?

Something else happened around the same time that I received the children's Bible. My mother took me to Christmas Eve worship at our neighbors' church. I do not remember much except how strange it was to see other kids from school and people from the community together in one place. I never thought that people I knew went to church.

I also recall how they treated my mother as we left the building after worship. My parents always struggled to pay the bills. We were the family that shopped for school clothes, furniture, and anything else we needed at garage sales. I was that kid at school who other kids mocked and bullied because he wore their cast-off clothes. In the community, my family was not the one people excitedly greeted to share the latest news and gossip. We were the town drunk's family. So, it surprised me when people said hello to my mother. They smiled at her with big, toothy grins. Some even shook her hand, and others hugged her. But these were the same people who, outside of church, bullied me and treated my family with contempt. It was a strange experience, and it did nothing to get me excited about church.

Although I only attended worship one time as a child, every year around Christmas God would preach the good news about Jesus Christ to me. He used Linus, who stood on that stage with the rest of the *Peanuts* gang and proclaimed the Christmas message from Luke's gospel to every person in the world who had tuned in to watch *A Charlie Brown Christmas*. There were moments like this, and there were people God used to get the gospel into my ears. I see that now in hindsight. A children's Bible. A neighbor's invitation to attend Christmas worship. Even a cartoon character. Eventually, I started to think a bit more seriously about what it all meant. But instead of going to church, I went to a library.

As an adolescent, I was obsessed with fantasy novels and comic books. In high school, I studied witchcraft and folk religions. In college, I went even further. I studied mythology, folklore, shamanism, and the like. My lifelong fascination with philosophy and the hard sciences also began. Camus's *The Myth of Sisyphus* and Hawking's *A Brief History of Time* captured my imagination. From there I dove into Plato and Taoism, microbiology and quantum mechanics. This was when I turned an intellectual corner. As I went deeper and deeper into the data about mitochondria and quarks, it caused me to wonder: Is everything an accident, a random sequence of events without purpose or meaning, or is there more to life, the universe, and everything? The ways and workings of the world are just too elegant, I thought. It is all too elegant to be a series of mathematically incomprehensible accidents. Some higher power or personality must be at work. The elegance of a cell convinced me there was a God, but I could still hear my father's voice saying, "If there's a God, then why did those 99 men die?"

Eventually, I did conclude that there must be a God, but I still had my doubts. At the same time, I occasionally attended worship during the holidays with my girlfriend's family—not because I wanted to, but because she did. I was a teenage boy. I had one thing on my mind, and it was not God. This was a constant theme, like it or not, that would bring me into churches up to my conversion. The only way I could be motivated to go to church on Sunday was because a girlfriend attended worship. But since God is not above employing a donkey to proclaim the gospel, young lust was certainly not going to get in the way of his preaching to me. In whatever way he wanted to smuggle the gospel to me, he did it.

What do you do when you start to believe there is a God but still have doubts? I talked to Christian friends, but they were not helpful. They wanted to talk about Jesus. I wanted to talk about God in the language of science and philosophy. I moved on from Christian friends to friends who embraced the teachings of the Buddha and some who described themselves as spiritual but not religious. Some were into shamanistic practices, and one was raised an observant Jew. The more we talked, the more convinced I was that their beliefs provided a justification for their lifestyle. Their beliefs did not necessarily shape their values, but their values definitely seemed to shape their beliefs. These conversations, as frustrating as they were for me at the time, spurred me on to seek out holy books for what I hoped would give me a better way to God. I started with the Bhagavad Gita and the teachings of the Buddha. Then I moved to the Tao Te Ching. (I enjoyed it so much that I memorized it.) Then I read the Qur'an, Jewish Midrash, and any sacred text I could purchase at the local used bookstore. At the end of three months, there was not much left on the shelf because I had bought almost all of them. All except one—the *Oxford Annotated Bible*.

I made a run at being a Buddhist. That lasted a while, but drug addiction made it difficult to meditate. I tried to follow the teachings of Islam for two or three months. There were too many rules. I was too impatient to really meditate on the Tao and apply its wisdom to my life. Judaism did not appeal to me. Again, there were too many rules. Christianity was a non-starter. I knew Christians. I was not impressed by their defense of the faith or the way they used forgiveness as a cover to "live like a rock star," as we liked to say. They were right there with me, living like a rock star, so I took a hard pass on getting too involved with more Christians. This meant I was stuck. I had come to believe in God through science and philosophy, which was not the way other people I knew had come to believe. They had either been born into their religion or come to faith in junior high or high school by way of youth retreats and mission-outreach projects. I had not enjoyed any of those experiences. That meant, on the one hand, I could not rely on experience to help me answer my questions about God. On the other hand, I was not convinced anything I had read was pointing me to some set of transcendent truths about God that would satisfy my questions. Out of options and feeling like I was in the middle of a psychotic break, I pushed aside my prejudice (for the moment) and purchased a Bible.

The first thing I noticed about the *Oxford Annotated Bible* was its size. It was so large. I didn't know where to begin. Since I was familiar with the Old Testament from my children's Bible, I decided to start in Genesis. But by chapter five I was bored. Then, when I paged through the book and discovered it was 60 chapters long, I gave up on it. I tried to read Exodus, but it seemed like more of the same—too long and, from what little I read, too boring.

I paged through the Bible to find a book that was not as long and boring as Genesis and Exodus. (I figured out from the table of contents that a Bible is not one long story but 66 different stories.) The other books of Moses were a non-starter. They were too long. Judges was too bloody. The history of the Kings bored me. The Psalms confused me. Is God my help, or has he given me over to my enemies? The prophets were long-winded and unfathomable. The minor prophets were angry and incomprehensible. I turned to the New Testament. I began to read Matthew's gospel, but Jesus seemed too angry and judgmental. I took a shot at Mark's gospel. It was more of the same. Why was Jesus so grumpy all the time? I tried to read Acts, but it made no sense. I found Philemon, and it was just the right length. But I could not figure out what anything in the letter had to do with my questions about God. Finally, I came to 1 John. Here was a letter that was not too long. There was a lot of weird love talk, but also a lot of God talk. This might be the one!

When I read 1 John 4, all my circuits blew. This was something I had not read in any of the other religious texts. It was not a list of dos and don'ts I have to complete if I want to be saved. For the first time, I didn't feel the hand-wringing worries about whether God is even paying attention to me or the persistent wonder over whether I had done enough to please him. I encountered a simple statement that changed everything for me:

> *Beloved, let us love one another, for love is from God, and whoever loves has been born of God and knows God. Anyone who does not love does not know God, because God is love. In this the love of God was made manifest among us, that God sent his only Son into the world, so that we might live through him. In this is love, not that we have loved God but that he loved us and sent his Son to be the propitiation for our sins (1 John 4:7–10).*

Love. What I learned from John's letter was the first time I had read anything that described God and love in the same breath.

God loves me? God did that for me? And what is this about his Son? Propitiation? Maybe I had read Matthew's gospel the wrong way. Maybe I had missed the point of the Bible. Maybe I needed to reconsider what the essential teachings of all the religions I had studied were, because they did not seem to line up with what I was reading in 1 John. Maybe I had found an answer to my questions about God?

I asked my Christian friends about this and where I could find help to understand what John had described. They pointed me to C. S. Lewis's *Mere Christianity*. I purchased it, devoured it, and devoted myself to reading everything I could lay my hands on by him. He did help me. He gave me language to describe my experience, since he had gone through a similar route from unbelief to faith. He pointed me to God's love, what part Jesus played in expressing that love, and where I might go to enjoy God's love. That meant going back to church.

I attended a Catholic mass for Easter. I about choked to death on incense smoke. I have witnessed house fires that put out less smoke than what erupted from that brazier. After that, I went to worship at a Lutheran church with some girlfriends. The experience did not make Christianity better for me, but it did manage to make rock music worse. But I was going to follow Lewis's advice. I was going to go to church. I would hear God's Word preached. I would worship with other believers. I would devote myself to daily prayer and reading the Bible. I would change my life. I wanted the concrete, real love of God I had read about in 1 John. The problem was that I just could not manage to find it at any of the churches I attended. The churches, like the sacred texts I had read, seemed more concerned about what I was doing to please God than what God was doing to love me.

At the time, it seemed that Christianity offered me more of the same. In the marketplace of religions, here was just one more vendor. Buddhism, Islam, new age spirituality, and Christianity all seemed to share common characteristics. Stripped down to their essential parts, religions seemed to offer a seeker very much the same set of core doctrines. It was only the outward expression of these doctrines that differed.

Up until this point, what I learned from all the religions I studied was essentially this: there is divinity, whether a god, goddess, or multitude of gods. This divine being, or beings, created everything that exists. Creation usually involved separation—light and dark, water and dirt, order and chaos, gods and human beings. Sometimes creation was the result of a war between old and new gods. At other times, creation was simply what happened when the earth emerged from an infinite sea when the sun rose for the first time. Most of the time, though, a central theme in any creation myth is violence, of order overcoming chaos. It was violence that brought the universe into existence. Violence forms the subtext of all divine and human experiences. Violence shapes the relation between a god, or gods, and people.

What I heard in the churches on Sunday morning, about God's Spirit hovering over the chaos, separation of light and dark, water and dirt, the creation of people, all sounded similar to what I had learned from the creation mythos of other religions. There was violence, too, especially when Adam and Eve took the forbidden fruit and ate. They rebelled against the will of God. They were naked and afraid of God's anger. They were punished by God with earthly torture and eternal death. But something rubbed me wrong about the events of Genesis 3. There was something odd about it. Despite what seemed to be more of the same, there was something that pushed itself to the front of the narrative that distinguished itself from the other sacred texts. In spite of his creation's rebellion, God seemed more focused on saving his people from their rebellion and subsequent enslavement to sin and death. He seemed more concerned about saving rather than punishing his creation.

Other religions marked humanity's "fall" as our failure to pass the test. That is, we are put on earth by the gods to serve them in what ends up being a test called "life." Depending on how we perform in our service to the gods, we get rewarded with paradise and eternal celebration or punished with hell and eternal torture. It all depends, in the end, on how we exercise our (free) will. Our eternal destiny depends on how we choose to obey or disobey the gods.

In the Genesis narrative, however, things played out differently. In spite of Adam and Eve's rebellion—they took what was not given to them—God seemed more intent on restoration than damnation. But there was plenty of blame to go around. There were plenty of opportunities to bring divine wrath down on their heads. The serpent persuaded the woman that God was holding something back from them—the knowledge of good and evil.

When they ate the fruit and their eyes were opened, they were not overjoyed at the knowledge of good and evil. They did not rejoice at being like God. They were ashamed. Naked and vulnerable, they tried to cover themselves. They saw and heard and felt a threat to their lives everywhere. Even the wind inspired terror. Was that God? Was he coming to kill them?

Adam and Eve tried to protect themselves from each other, from other creatures, and even from their Creator. He did say that when they ate the fruit they would die. What else could God have meant other than he would kill them? So, when they heard God walking in the garden, they did the equivalent of fashioning tinfoil hats for themselves so that God could not see their thoughts—they hid behind some trees. Why? Because, as we all know, nothing will throw off the Creator of more than 140 billion galaxies like hiding behind some shrubbery. But did God threaten them if they did not show themselves? No, he called to the man, "Adam, where are you?" When the man showed himself, all he could think to do was throw Eve under the bus: "It was the woman you gave to me. She gave me the fruit and I ate it." But did God turn and obliterate the woman from existence? No. He listened. He asked questions. Then the woman, to divert blame, pointed out that it was all the serpent's doing. But did God devour the serpent in a fit of rage? No. He listened to the man and woman. In the end, he listened to them invent religion.

Look closer at Genesis 3, though, and something else sticks out. One could argue that God cut off Adam's attempt to create a religion before it gained any traction. Just look at how it all goes down. Adam and Eve rebel. Adam tries to sacrifice Eve to save himself. Eve argues that the serpent should take her punishment. But what does God do? He used Eve's womb against the serpent. The serpent had attempted to weaponize Eve's womb against God. If the man and woman died, as God promised, then that would have meant no babies. No babies would mean God's plan for his creation would be undone before it even began. But now, instead of creation being undone through Eve's rebellion, God would regenerate and renew creation by way of Eve's child. The serpent might bite Eve's child, poisoning the boy with his venom, but the child would crush his skull.

CHAPTER 3

OUR GODS ARE EXPRESSIONS OF SIN

When I began to read seriously about the Christian faith, I first went to C.S. Lewis' *Mere Christianity*. I also read Augustine's *Confessions*. The two books seemed ubiquitous; they were in the library of every one of my Christian friends. I first read Lewis and Augustine sitting on the floor of my apartment in St. Paul, Minnesota. I also took them with me during my time serving as a music teacher at an orphanage in Vicente Guerrero, Baja California. And, from there, I carried them with me into a meeting with a pastor in Portland, Oregon. He would go on to mentor me in the faith and lay the groundwork for me to attend seminary.

It was Pastor Stephen Krueger who listened to my questions, absorbed my counter-attacks when he said something I disagreed with, and picked up the check for lunch. More importantly, he introduced me to Martin Luther. After a three-hour lunch conversation where I would lob questions at him, and he would volley answers back at me, Steve finally said, "You know, Donavon, you sound just like someone else I know who wrestled with similar questions. If you're open to a suggestion, I'd like to give you some books written by Martin Luther."

That lunch conversation introduced me to Martin Luther's works, and it was not long before I fell deeply in love with the sixteenth century German theologian. I also made up my mind at that time, especially after reading Luther's *Small Catechism*, that I would follow him wherever he wanted to lead me. So it goes to this day.

Luther's works are a theological gold mine. I found his contrast between true and false gods and the distinction he draws between the God who hides himself and the one who reveals himself in Jesus Christ to be the most profound. For example, in the *Small Catechism* he says that a god is whatever we fear, love, and trust above all things. When the true God shows up, we treat him like he is one more contestant in the divine beauty pageant. We fear the death of a child. We love that child more than ourselves. We trust that the child will be there every day, and eventually he or she will bury us. We fear, love, and trust in the longevity of our children more than God. We fear, love, and trust abstractions like wealth, fame, and power more than God, too. Whatever keeps us up at night, we turn into a god. We worship it. We submit to it. We sacrifice things to it. That is the depth of our selfishness.

This is what the Bible calls sin, and it runs deep within each and every one of us. We are so self-centered, that it is impossible for us to distinguish the true God from the people and things we fear, love, and trust most. All we have to do is step back, detach, and observe how our fears, loves, and dependence on things determine our choices for us before we even think to make a choice.

When I came to believe in God, it was a belief based on signs and explanations provided for me from science and philosophy. The material that brought me to the conclusion that there was a divine creator did not give me any specific information with which to work. The mechanisms of control by which God oversees life, the universe, and everything were not yet cemented for me. I believed there was a God, but which religion's God was the true God? They cannot all be the true God, can they? Which God is the true God? How does God want to be worshiped? Does God want to be worshiped? Do I have to change my life to serve God? What does that look like? I had a lot of questions, and every religious text I read seemed to say, "We are right. Everyone else is wrong." That is, until I read Luther's explanation of what he called the hidden and revealed God.

In Luther's debate with the famous Renaissance humanist, Erasmus of Rotterdam, he asserted that there is a place where God wants to be preached, revealed, and worshiped. There is also a place where God does not want to be preached, revealed, and worshiped. Where God reveals himself to us, he wants us to know him as a God who is for us. He loves and favors us. He works for our good, protects us from evil, and bends all creation toward our salvation. But we are to have nothing to do with what God has not revealed to and for us. That god, the one who is not preached, revealed, and worshiped in a specific way, is the god of every religion ever invented. Or to be more specific, according to Luther's reading of the Bible, whatever we know about God apart from how he reveals himself to us in in the person and work of Jesus Christ is up for debate. Outside Jesus, God may or may not be at work for us, but we have no way of knowing for certain. And whoever or whatever God is or isn't, apart from Jesus he is not the God who is for us in the way of forgiveness, life, and salvation.

That is really what distinguishes the God of Abraham, Isaac, and Jacob from all those other gods. The God of the patriarchs reveals himself to be God for us. He is not removed from creation. He is intimately caught up in it. God is in love with his creation. He creates because he is love and life. God did not create us to be slaves; he created us as his beloved children. We are meant to walk in freedom, not slavery. The life God gives us is not a test that needs to be passed. It is a love affair. It is a celebration of the relationship between Creator and creature. But all this is believed and confessed by Christians because of Jesus.

Jesus reveals the truth about God to us and the falsehood of our need to invent gods for every occasion.

Jesus reveals God to us, and he reveals sin to us, too. We may know by nature that there is a god, but we do not know by nature that our selfish nature is what the Bible calls sin. Why does this matter though? What does sin have to do with our belief in the true God? It is our selfish need to find purpose and meaning for our lives that drives us to invent gods. Why did that baby girl die in a car crash but that South American dictator just keeps on going? Why am I on my third marriage? Why did our crop fail? Why did the bank foreclose on the house? There must be a reason. There must be an explanation. There must be some greater meaning to what happens, and I better figure it out!

What Jesus reveals about God and our gods is that our gods are a projection of our values. The God of Abraham, Isaac, and Jacob, as Jesus proves time and again in the gospels, stands all our values on their head. He upends our ideals about what a god must be. He takes all our judgments about faith and life to the hill of Calvary and nails them to the cross. Jesus's death reveals something to us that we do not want to comprehend. Our relation to God is out of whack, and there is nothing we can do to fix it. In fact, the more we try to repair the relationship, the more uncertain we are about the status of our relationship to God. And inevitably we make things worse. Our gods are as distant, dispassionate, and impersonal as the future. The more we pursue them, the further away they appear. Jesus, on the other hand, is Emmanuel, God with us. We do not have to pursue him. Jesus comes from the future to seek and save the lost. We do not have to find him. He finds us, and he introduces himself to us in a specific way, at a specific time, in a specific place in the present. And that is at the root of our problem with the way God chooses to reveal himself to us.

When I was on the hunt for data about God, it wasn't the ideas that my intellect discovered but Jesus who provided the answer to my questions. Jesus is specific. He is, in the truest sense of the word, unique. Jesus is not presented in the gospels as a religious guru. He is not depicted as a moral reformer. He does not lead us to or open the way for us to know God. This man, Jesus, is God himself.

The specific way in which the gospels and epistles portray Jesus, especially with regard to the love of God, was so definite. It left me with no options. There was nothing about Jesus that needed further definition. I did not have to rummage around in my brain for categories in which to confine Jesus. Here was God described in a way that upended the way I thought about divinity. I had a loose set of criteria for what a god is and is not. The more I read the Bible, the more Jesus did not fit the bill. For this reason, too, I resonated with the religious leaders, crowds, and even Jesus's disciples, who were always quick to remind Jesus that he might be from God, but he cannot be God. He just does not talk or behave like a proper god. The difference, though, between myself and the leaders, crowds, and disciples was that the more I learned from pastors, Christian friends, and theologians, the more convinced I was that I shared Thomas's post-resurrection confession about Jesus. Through those people, He brought me to faith. He led me to see that Jesus actually is my Lord and my God.

All the other religions I had studied had it wrong. God is not impersonal. The future is not something to be dreaded. Avoidance of death is not the purpose and goal of life. Jesus is not a projection of our emotional instability. Instead, according to the biblical witness, God comes closer to me than my next breath. The future has come ahead of time, in the affirmative, to announce God's promised redemption of all creation. Death, like sin, is overcome and defeated by Jesus.

The thing I had been looking for was specificity. I did not want generic answers to my questions about God. I wanted details. But ultimately, I wanted someone or something to explain how I could believe in God yet not want to believe. In the gospels, not only was I introduced to people who had the same problem; I was also given, along with them, a resolution in the person of Jesus.

And, in Paul's letter to the Romans 7:22–8:4 I received a beautiful summation, the specific answer I had hoped for:

> *So, I find it to be a law that when I want to do right, evil lies close at hand. For I delight in the law of God, in my inner being, but I see in my members another law waging war against the law of my mind and making me captive to the law of sin that dwells in my members. Wretched man that I am! Who will deliver me from this body of death? Thanks be to God through Jesus Christ our Lord! So then, I myself serve the law of God with my mind, but with my flesh I serve the law of sin. There is therefore now no condemnation for those who are in Christ Jesus. For the law of the Spirit of life has set you free in Christ Jesus from the law of sin and death. For God has done what the law, weakened by the flesh, could not do. By sending his own Son in the likeness of sinful flesh and for sin, he condemned sin in the flesh, in order that the righteous requirement of the law might be fulfilled in us, who walk not according to the flesh but according to the Spirit.*

That was what I had wanted to hear all along! I did not need more people to tell me that there was a God. I did not need more information about how I could work my way into God's good graces. I just wanted clarity. I wanted someone to say to me, "The reason you do not want to believe, even though you believe, is because you don't have it in you to believe in God. God's faithfulness, not your faith, is what creates and nurtures belief." And here, finally, was Jesus. Here, in the letter to the Romans, was my release from confusion and doubt. And, as Paul wrote to another group of believers struggling to live in the Gospel and not return to self-salvation projects: "The Son of God loved me, and gave himself for me" (Galatians 2:20).

The one who was before Abraham, and who existed before the world was created, is God. God's Word, Jesus, created everything, and there is nothing that he did not create. His death saves us all from death. But how do we know this to be true? Only God, who is seen through Jesus' suffering and death on the cross, is the true God. God does not want us to know him in any other way than in the way Jesus reveals God to us. God wants to be known to us, not in the way we imagine God to be, but in the event of the crucifixion of Jesus. God shows himself to us in a specific way, at a specific time, in a specific place so that we can know where to find him. We cannot know God from our side of the street. He has to come to us, speak to us, and introduce himself to us. The way God did this is through Jesus' suffering and death. Jesus' works and words open for us the way to knowledge about God. Here we are confronted by a concrete, real, historical event. Jesus was an actual man. He really did live, and suffer, and was executed. He rose from the dead three days later. He appeared to his disciples and over five hundred people. As Paul put it, so that we might have assurance all that he taught was true (Acts 17:31).

Jesus puts us at a crossroads. Do we go where he leads us, or do we run to other gods? If we go where he leads, we go to Calvary. If we run from him, we end up back in the chaos of our emotions, anxious about what tomorrow may bring. But to be in relation to Jesus, in the specific way he reveals his divinity to us, we are connected to what Luther called the theology of the cross. This is shorthand for how God reveals himself to us in shame, ruin, death, and everything that is put on display for the world to see in the suffering of Jesus. To prove himself to be God, God chooses to present himself in a way that flies in the face of all human wisdom and understanding about what makes a god a god. In this way, there can be no confusion about the true God and the gods we invent for ourselves.

The biblical witness to Jesus was my end point. I had the data I needed. It provoked, challenged, and confounded me. More importantly, it distinguished Jesus from all the other religious teachers. Moses, Muhammad, and the Buddha pointed to their god, but they were not God. Other religious gurus taught how to escape this catastrophic reality. Most laid out a heroic narrative for achieving success, how to gain heaven while avoiding hell, but that, in the end, was what led me to confess Jesus as Savior and God.

Every religion has at its heart a heroic narrative. Some super-manly warrior god, a beautiful yet deadly sword-wielding god-dess, or a brave human champion who overcomes great adversity and completes a heroic quest to save his people. They are not too different than the stories found in comic books.

Take Superman, for example. While the story was created by authors familiar with biblical heroes (Jerry Siegel and Joel Shuster were Jewish), their motivation came from a deeper, more painful place. Jerry Siegel's father had been fatally shot by a rob-ber. At the same time this happened, in the 1930s, America was suffering through the Great Depression, and the world was just waking up to was happening in Nazi Germany. People were look-ing for a savior, in a person they could look up to, who would inspire them and in whom they could hope. Superman was one such savior—the savior Siegel and Shuster believed the world needed. Superman saved fathers from being shot to death. He saved people from crushing hunger and illness. He rescued inno-cent people from the schemes of evil men, just like (Siegel and Shuster believed) Samson and Moses did for Israel.

Siegel and Shuster tapped into a fear all people experience at one time or another. We are not in control of what happens to us. We are vulnerable. At any moment, forces beyond our power and comprehension can take away our job, our well-being, and our life. At those times, who will save us? We need a hero, an other-worldly force for good. We need a heroic figure. One who comes from above. One sent by the heavenly father to save the Earth. Then, when he comes down to Earth, he is raised by two human parents, Martha and Jonathan (who, by the way, originally had the names Mary and Joseph). And at age thirty, he leaves home to engage in his public mission. This super-warrior—this savior of the world—will fight for the biblical principles of truth and justice. And just when you think he is dead he explodes from the grave! He rises from death to overcome the chaotic forces of evil that tried to destroy him.

That is the god we want. We want a Superman kind of god. But the truth is, as much as we want a hero like Superman to rescue us from evil and death, that is not what God gives us. Sure, there are similarities between the Superman narrative and what the gospels communicate to us about Jesus. Siegel and Shuster were Jewish, after all, and Jesus is the subject of "all the Law and the prophets." But where Superman and Jesus part ways is in the way the gospels portray our Savior. Jesus is not Superman. He is not from another planet. He is from Earth. He does not possess powers far beyond those of mortal men. No. Instead, Jesus is just as ordinary as anybody else. Most important, he is born, lives, and dies a Clark Kent kind of guy. And when Jesus comes out of the tomb, he is still Clark Kent. There is no red cape or blue tights; no heat vision or cold breath; no alter-ego. He is not faster than a speeding bullet, more powerful than a locomotive, or able to leap tall buildings in a single bound. From beginning to end, Jesus is just a plain-old Clark Kent kind of man.

This is at the root of the biblical witness of who God is for us and who we are in relation to God. We want to be more than human. We want to be god in God's place, or at least little gods. And if that is not possible, then we want to live that unachievable reality vicariously through our Christ-figures. We want heroes we can never be to inspire us to be more human than human. We want to escape our humanity. We do not enjoy the inescapable reality of shame, vulnerability, and weakness. But from what we learn about Jesus, God does not want to lift us up out of our humanity. He becomes a man to restore our lost humanity.

Superman is exactly who Jesus is not. Jesus is the very human child who "grew in wisdom and stature, who enjoyed the favor of God and men" (Luke 2:52). He is the man from Nazareth, Joseph's son, who gathered students to himself and taught them the way of God's kingdom before his brutal torture at the hands of Roman soldiers.

It is difficult for us to accept that Jesus was an ordinary man. We are happy to play around with what it means that Jesus was and is God, but his humanity presents us with problems. Who wants to be reminded that he came to save us in our humanity, not help us escape from it? Nobody. We want Jesus to come and save us from being ordinary, from just being human.

That is why Jesus was crucified. He was not executed because he was God, or because he blasphemed against God, even though the religious leaders tried to frame it this way to justify their blood lust. Jesus was crucified because he claimed to be God, but he did not live up to anyone's standards of what a proper god must be. It is not that we do not want a Savior; it is just that Jesus is not the kind of Savior we look for or want.

Our kind of Savior would come down off his cross. He would carry a folding phone booth in his back pocket. He would not do a stupid thing like rise from the dead. He would avoid suffering and dying in the first place. That way—with him as the kind of Savior we want—we would not have to worry about suffering and death either.

If we are trying to imagine what it is like for God to be a man, it is not just hard. It is impossible. We can stop trying to imagine what it was like for Jesus. Just know that he thought, and spoke, and experienced feelings like us, because that is exactly how the Bible describes Jesus' humanity. Jesus was perfectly ordinary in every way.

Jesus did not change water into wine, raise the dead, or exorcize demons because he had superpowers. He did it all by God's grace that comes through the work of the Holy Spirit. Likewise, Jesus was not driven into the wilderness to fast and pray because he was possessed by some high-octane spiritual gas. The Spirit drove him into the wilderness. When Jesus was little, he did not figure out Aramaic or carpentry or learn the Hebrew Bible because he was superhuman. If he received any heavenly help, it was the Holy Spirit who did it all. This is the same Spirit we receive on account of our baptism into Christ Jesus.

Yes, Jesus is God, and he knows how to save us. But he becomes just as we are so he is able to sympathize with us in every way, especially in our suffering, temptations, and death. And even though he is not the Savior we want Jesus is the Savior we need. He does not save us from suffering and death. He is there with us in the hurt, the damage, the shame, and the doubts. He speaks to us, feeds us, and walks with us through the messes we have made of our life. By the grace of God, he knows how to bring us comfort, peace, and hope in the power of his resurrection. This is the God-man, Jesus the Christ.

What the Bible teaches us, then, is that the long-awaited Savior of the nations is no Superman. He is just an unimpressive, unremarkable, Clark-Kent kind of man. That is how our God reveals himself to us. He is the incarnate and human God, Jesus the Christ, who "had to be made like his brothers in every respect, so that he might become a merciful and faithful high priest in the service of God, to make propitiation for the sins of the people" (Hebrews 2:17).

CHAPTER 4

JESUS IS THE END
OF RELIGION

My first full exposure to what I call "hardcore Christianity" was in the mission field. I lived among born-again Christians in Mexico. I was, for the most part, just like them, too. Whatever we may have disagreed upon as far as theology or living out our faith was concerned, the common thread that ran through every person's autobiography was that we were misfits—former unbelievers, alcoholics, and drug addicts that had hit rock bottom. We did not fit in anywhere. That is why I found myself at the mission. Just like the people who were already there, or who arrived after me, we hungered and thirsted for fellowship as much as righteousness. We had serious faith questions and an urgency about us. We looked at our neighbors back home, family and friends, and concluded that they were too lackadaisical about being Christian.

For me, though, the feeling of not fitting in was amplified through my study of philosophy and religious teachings. I realized that the one-size-fits-all solution offered by philosophy and religious teachings—do good if you want to save yourself from earthly and divine judgment—was essentially a call to be a well-behaved toy that knows its place in relation to all the other toys. I was taught to go with the religious flow, so to speak, but I always seemed to be swimming against the current.

Even though I was now a Christian, I still had lots of issues. I knew my daily schedule of alcohol and drugs, lies and deceptions were not God's purpose for me. So, I confessed my sins at church every Sunday morning, but then went right back to life as usual. This only drove me deeper into anxiety and frustration. I needed more than one hour of "God time" each week. I needed to devote every moment to God's service. *Maybe that way*, I thought, *I will get the peace for which I've searched and prayed.*

That is how I ended up in Mexico teaching music and choir at an orphanage. I also played in praise bands at the local church. I volunteered at the mission's free clinic. I jumped at every chance to go into the field with the outreach team. I helped build a rehabilitation center for alcoholics and drug addicts. Whatever I could do to drive away the sense that I did not measure up to God's standards of what a Christian is supposed to be, I said yes. How could I not? I was now in a place, both personally and geographically, where I was convinced God was either going to throw me back into the ditch of addiction or hoist me up and make me a righteous man.

I was taught to read the Bible every day. I was taught to pray all the time. Anything that did not praise God was to be thrown away—no movies, television, or music that was not specifically Christian. I was to only form relationships with other Christians, and if I met an unbeliever it was imperative that I preach hell to them until they repented and accepted Jesus as their Savior.

Everything about my life as a missionary was tailored to fight the good fight of faith. I got up before the sun to attend prayer circles. I went to bed late, because I did not want to leave Bible study and fellowship events too early, afraid I might miss something important. Every morning we gathered after breakfast for chapel. We did everything together to encourage and build each other up to serve God. It seemed at the time like the perfect place for someone like me who did not grow up in church to learn the basic tenets of Christianity.

The problem was that the more I focused my attention on godly behavior, changing the way I spoke, acted, and thought, the more apparent it was that I had failed to live a godly life. I did not know whether I believed Jesus was God. I rejected God as my Father, since my own father was such a solid brass bastard. If God was just a bigger version of my biological father, I was going to take a hard pass. I did not understand how Jesus, who died in the past, could be of any use to me in the present tense. The people I lived alongside of were damaged, some profoundly hurt and harmed by their own hand. And as I learned, for all their talk of godly faith and obedience, they sinned as much (or worse) in private as any unbeliever I partied with in college.

In fact, the more I tried to change, the more apparent it was to me that I fell far, far short of being a Christian worthy of God's attention. After three months at the mission, I was sure I had made a terrible mistake. Not only did I not feel closer to God, but I also believed I was doomed. God had pulled me out of my unbelief and brought me to Mexico, and now I had to suffer in silence the rest of my life, knowing what waited for me at the Judgment Day. I was damned.

The more I tried to curb my tongue, change my behavior, and realign my thoughts with those of Jesus, Paul, or the theologians I read, the more obvious it was that sin had its hooks in me and was not going on vacation anytime soon. For example, I prayed that God would take away the cravings. But at night in bed, I would plot out how I would take a microbus to the next town over where nobody knew me so I could drink. I prayed God would take away my lust. But I prayed that he would not do it just yet. I met a young woman who was just as excited as me to sneak into the orchard at night to make out in secret under the almond trees. I liked the blues and rock music. I enjoyed secular movies. Most of all, I wrestled against the assertion that if I did not live the right kind of life, God would abandon me.

I did not want to believe in God, at least not the Christian God. That is why, every time the pastor or some elder said, "If you talk this way . . ." or "If you do this . . ." or "If you allow your- selves to think about that you are not living a Christian life,"

I took those as invitations to escape not just the mission but belief altogether. Every prohibition and every "if . . . then" statement convinced me I could out-sin God's grace. If I could just do enough sin, maybe he would throw me back into the ditch where he had found me. In this way, I could escape the daily torture that came with hiding my deep, dark secret: God was good and righteous and I was not. I did not deserve to be called a Christian.

Before I was a Christian, I believed I was doomed. Now, I was a Christian (sort of), and I was convinced beyond all doubt that I was doomed. That is when I realized I would rather burn out on drugs and alcohol, and all the chaos that came with them, than to drift toward judgment and damnation as a Sunday pew sitter.

That does not mean I did not enjoy the people. I came to love many of the people at the mission—Doctor Marco Angulo and his family, who took me in and gave me their name, the orphans who taught me Spanish, and the house parents, pastors, and other missionaries. They walked with me and helped me. They taught me to revere God's Word. They taught me to pray, praise, and give thanks to God for everything. And, as odd as it may seem after what I have written thus far, I would have stayed there for the rest of my life if I had the chance, because, despite my struggles, I felt safe. I was loved. (Plus, I was in Mexico near the beach, and I could surf every day.)

But there was just no getting past the doubt. The more I changed, the more apparent my sin became. I needed Jesus as my Savior, but every day I seemed to push him further away from me into the anxious future. I fought the good fight of faith, but I kept getting knocked down by sin, worldly temptations, and the accusations of the evil one. I played, sang, taught, volunteered, studied, prayed, and dedicated my every waking moment to glorifying God with my life, and I was miserable. I was a dry drunk. I was a grumpy Christian. I was driven by my cravings. I was permanently damaged. And the constant reminder of "God loves you" was not cutting it. I needed more than pablum. I needed that spiritual meat the apostle Paul referred to in his first letter to the Corinthian church. I needed more from Christianity than, "Believe in God, be a good Christian, and know that God loves you."

While I needed more, more was not what I got. Instead, more of the same is what I got. So, I left the mission. I intended to return after the new year, once I had had time to think and work out some questions for myself, but the way back was blocked. Instead of going back to Mexico for the rest of my life, I ended up in Portland, Oregon, for three years. It was there that the "more" I craved was offered to me.

I mentioned the pastor ho mentored me in the faith in the first chapter. Through him, the good Lord gave me the more I craved. He led me to the gospel and His gifts. I was introduced to the specific "for-youness" of the preached gospel. I was directed to focus my attention on where Jesus makes himself present for his people—in the gospel, baptism, and the Lord's Supper. I was taught that his gifts do what he says they do. They forgive sin, strengthen faith, increase love, and produce hope in the Christian. What I yearned for—and what was missing until I met Pastor Steven Kreuger in Portland—was a present-tense declaration of forgiveness that carried God's real, concrete promise and power to change my heart with it.

Until then I had heard about what Jesus did in the past. I was warned about what would happen in the future when Jesus returned. But what was notably absent from so many sermons, Bible studies, and conversations was the present-tense effect God's Word and Spirit had in the life of each believer. I was completely unprepared to hear someone say to me, "In the name of Jesus, I forgive all your sin." The first time the pastor said it, I asked, "What do you mean?" He responded, "Jesus died for your sin, and therefore you are forgiven. Because God made him to be sin so that you may become the righteousness of God." It only took me another two years of constant conversation with my pastor to begin to grasp the enormity of what he had said to me. But I was not going anywhere. I wanted all that he had to give in the way of preaching a present-tense gospel.

Pastor Kreuger introduced me to Martin Luther and Lutheran theology. He fed me a steady diet of theology and Christian history from the early church to modern theologians. He prepared me to preach and teach Bible class. He convinced me to attend seminary. Twenty years later, as I write this, he still stands as a beacon of God's grace toward me. When we first met, I was so depressed, so defeated by my engagements with churches and Christians that I had decided to give up altogether. Wherever I went, whatever church I attended, whichever Christians I interacted with, I just did not fit in. And I could not escape back to Mexico. When I was hopeless, that pastor invited me into his company, into the church he served, and into an amazing group of theologians who can be counted among the great cloud of witnesses to the truth about Jesus as Savior.

What was so amazing about my pastor's approach to theology was his insistence that Christianity is about Jesus and Jesus alone. It was not Jesus plus my ability to believe or Jesus plus my works. It was just Jesus, who took the work of salvation out of our hands.

Over the years, I had found that many Christians resist this good news. I have been laughed at, scorned, vilified and even had other Christians try to run me out of the ministry for refusing to move off the confession that we are justified before God by grace alone, through faith alone, in Christ alone apart from all our works. Why? Why is something that seems so obvious, so thoroughly biblical, treated as a threat in Christian churches? I believe it is because the confession of Jesus alone exposes us. Jesus' Good Friday passion reveals that we are unrepentantly religious. It is not that we are irreligious. It is because we hang on to the religion the old Adam. Rather than recognize the great gift who hangs crucified on Golgotha for the sin of the world, we turn away to look for something better. We look for a better God, and we find one closer to home. We find ourselves, rather than the one who is laid bare on the cross.

In our search for meaning, we do not take or look at ourselves too closely. Instead of a sinner who deserves God's wrath and punishment, we find who we imagine we are—a good, nice, godly person. This is what I had been taught was Christianity until I landed in Portland. It was religion slathered with "Jesus talk." "Believe in God, go to church on Sunday, behave yourselves, and you will go to heaven when you die." It turned out the thing that had turned me off to other religions, and what had driven me into such a funk about Christianity, was basically the same thing.

When Christianity becomes just one more religion in the marketplace of religions Jesus fades into the background. Is Jesus important? Yes, of course. Is Jesus the Savior of the world? Yes, according to the Bible. But so far as what Jesus does in the present tense, apart from what we do or make of him, that is where things get murky. When Jesus fades into the background Christianity is reduced to a form of what has been dubbed moralistic therapeutic deism. Instead of Jesus, God in a general, abstract sense takes center stage. There is a God. God created the world and ordered everything according to his will. God wants us to be nice to each other. The purpose and goal of life is to be happy and love ourselves. In the present tense, God is only needed when we get in trouble. If we are good, we will go to heaven when we die. That is the sum and substance of all religions, with minor tweaks made here and there to account for personal, cultural, and historical context.

Moralistic therapeutic deism gets us off the hook.[2] This general, abstract belief in God saves us from having to take seriously the exclusive claims the Bible makes about Jesus as God and Savior. It gives us cover to live in a kind of theological relativism. Sin, death, and judgment are antiquated ideas. We often believe that God loves us just the way we are, and he would never judge us or send us to hell unless we were really, really bad, like Adolf Hitler bad. Even then, we prefer not to discuss sin and evil

[2] This term comes from the book, *Soul Searching: The Religious and Spiritual Lives of American Teenagers,* by sociologists Christian Smith and Melinda Lundquist Denton.

and hell, because they make us uncomfortable and may hurt our self-esteem. Worse yet, other people may think we are being judgmental or "judgy."

Moralistic therapeutic deism places an emphasis on individualistic faith. Belief is personal and private. How each person chooses to express their beliefs is their prerogative. People can get together to worship their God, but only so long as everyone understands that worship is a kind of social contract. We all agree that we want to worship our God together. We all agree to get along for an hour or two on Sunday. We agree to behave ourselves, put on our Sunday best clothes, and act out the previously agreed upon rituals. But we are all aware that whatever is to be gotten out of worship, whatever is meaningful for each believer, is personal. In fact, the only true sin in a church that has embraced moralistic therapeutic deism is for people to be too certain about their convictions, and to try to impose them on others.

At root, moralistic therapeutic deism is really about instruction in how to live a moral life. It preaches that God's will for our lives is that we be good and happy. To be a good Christian, then, means that we are nice people who are focused on personal growth and self-improvement. Growth and self-improvement, whether they are framed as growth in grace or the Spirit, are important because we should always be focused on being kinder, more respectful people. Likewise, we are to take seriously our mental, physical, and spiritual health. After all, how can we grow and improve if our personal lives are a train wreck of mental, physical, and spiritual illness? When we take care of ourselves, we are better able to help others. Finally, we do our best to be successful at whatever task we undertake. Why? Because our success allows us to live in relative safety, happiness, and peace with God and each other. Our success at being religious opens up more opportunities to add to and embellish our do-it-yourself religion.

For those who have grown up in a church, God-talk and theological conversations serve the purpose of further cementing the foundation of whatever religious shack they have built for themselves. Emphasis on individual faith and not being judgy toward others punctuates much of the Christianity I have encountered over the years. This is mirrored and has probably been learned from our broader culture. Believe in God and be nice to each other has become the post-modern Christian's version of the Golden Rule.

In this respect, then, any talk about God is kept abstract and vague so as not to challenge or offend other people, especially other believers. In this way, we end up with a God who is nonspecific and therefore inoffensive. He, she, or it is open to multiple definitions and meanings depending on the individual's present felt needs. Yes, there is a God. Yes, this God created all that exists. But God does not make demands of us so much as to offer encouragement like an over-anxious yoga instructor. Whatever God is to the individual believer, one thing is for sure. God is distant.

That is the way we want him. So long as God is not in our face, or closer, we have time and choice. These are the two most valued commodities to old Adam sinners: time to grow and improve and choices that open up a future of endless possibilities to us. This allows us the freedom, we imagine, to be our own savior. For Christians, this means that when we do talk about Jesus, he is not held up as our savior so much as a moral example we seek to emulate. We worship him as Savior only insofar as he serves as a kind of true north for our self-salvation projects.

When we frame Jesus this way, it also allows us to escape from the ghosts of churches past. No more do we have to worry about the almighty God of Job who thunders out of the whirlwind. There is no need to worry about the warrior God of Abraham, Joshua, and David. There is no need to worry about the Righteous Judge who haunted Luther's every moment in the monastery. We have progressed past such archaic beliefs. We know better now, that God just wants to help us out of trouble and make us happy.

This kind of God makes sense to us, even when we dress him up as Jesus. He demands nothing from us. He is always ready to answer our prayer. He would never judge us for our life choices. He is the perfect God for us—harmless, meaningless, and godless. Of course, this has proven fatal for Christian churches. When this ideology that masquerades itself as theology is embraced, Christianity becomes just another religion. Worse, Christianity becomes just another support group, comparable to any AA meeting.

We do this so naturally that it often goes unnoticed. We replace Christian theology and belief with our personal theology and beliefs. We want to be almighty. We want control of our destiny. We do not need to repent; we need treatment. We do not need forgiveness; we need help to become our true selves. We do not need God's Word, the creeds, or the faith "once delivered to the saints." We need happiness, safety, and meaning injected into our life. And if one church cannot produce these desired results, there are plenty of others.

For many Christians in American churches, this means they spend their lives as Lutheran, Presbyterian, Roman Catholic, or nondenominational but would feel equally at home in worship with Mormons or Jehovah's Witnesses. They believe in God, they are religious, they love a good praise song, and they just want to be happy. And this is made possible so long as they are not confronted with the biblical witness to Jesus, that his death and resurrection is the end of all religion, even the religion of nice, happy, well-behaved Christians.

The most "in your face" way Jesus upsets our nice, happy vision of Christianity can be found in the parable of the Pharisee and tax collector (Luke 18:9–14). Two men went into a temple to pray— one extravagantly, the other quietly. Simple enough. But Jesus' parable is not about prayer. It's not about humility, piety, or what we must do and leave undone to merit God's good graces either. Instead, Jesus' parable is about the end of religion as we imagine it. The parable is about the uselessness of doing all we can to get right with God. It's about how foolish it is for us to even try.

Jesus does not say, "You've been doing it wrong the whole time. Now, here's how to get this religion thing right." Instead, Jesus warns us to surrender our claim on all our religious beliefs. All the stuff we do to justify ourselves to God is unjustifiable. That is why Jesus points us to his birth, death, and resurrection. This is how God finds the lost, strengthens the weak, and raises the dead.

Let's set it in a more modern context. Let's replace the Pharisee and tax collector with two pastors. The one pastor is a good man. He is a law-abiding citizen. He is not lazy about his responsibilities. He is not a drunk, a womanizer, or a cheat. He does not take anything that he has not earned. He gives his time and attention to everyone, even people who are not members of his church. He is a fair man and shows respect to everyone. He is faithful to his wife. He is patient and kind to his children. He is the type of friend people can count on to show up for them.

He is nothing like the other pastor down the road. That man is the worst kind of pastor. He is popular with all the wrong kinds of people. He is often seen in their company at the local bar, laughing and carrying on as if they do not have a care in the world. The bar flies take selfies with him. He receives money from other churches to help his little congregation, some of them not even members of his church body. He takes handouts from neighbors. His car is twice as expensive as all the other cars in the church parking lot. On Sunday morning, no weak church coffee for him. Only the best imported coffee is allowed to touch his lips.

Consider, again, the first pastor. This man is not just good; he is religious. He is not falsely religious. He is not a hypocrite. He is praised by his congregation for his uprightness. He is self-disciplined. He is an example to other Christians of piety, faith, and humility. He fasts every Saturday night to prepare for Sunday communion. He even puts 15 percent of his salary back into the offering plate every year. He is the kind of pastor most congregations would take, no questions asked. Best of all, he knows to thank God for his happy life.

But what does Jesus say about this kind of pastor, this man who any congregation would praise God for if he were in the pulpit come Sunday? Jesus tells us that not only is he in bad shape—he is in a worse condition than the other pastor who is as rotten as they come. The other pastor, who is an embarrassment to his profession, who just walks into church and does nothing more than say he is a mess, is in better shape than a first ballot hall-of-fame pastor. Why?

Well, God is sitting there in his house, weaving all creation together. He is speaking all things into existence. He is bent over, concentrating on making the hairs on our head out of nothing. He is holding our ligaments and tendons together. He is reconciling street hookers with their estranged parents. He is dragging yet another drunk into rehab. He is giving a baby the strength to take her first steps. He is filling a doctor with wisdom to stitch up a gunshot wound, and on and on and on into eternity.

Then, in walk these two guys. The first pastor walks to the front of the church, kneels before the altar, holds up his hands, and says, "Lord, I've been living as you would have me live. I'm obedient to your commands. I produce fruits of the Spirit. I do all that's expected of me, unlike that pastor down the road. I thank you that I have such a good life. Now, I know I strayed a bit yesterday. Please, help me get back on the right path." But rather than delight, God looks at the first pastor with a sad smile. He pushes down the pastor's hands and says, "Maybe your life isn't so good. Maybe you've never been on the right path at all."

The pastor raises his hands again. He says, "Okay. Maybe I didn't express myself the best way. Look, what I mean is, I've been devoted to you my whole life. I've obeyed your will as best I can, and I know you've blessed me because of it. All I'm asking is you help me get back on track so I can keep doing what needs to be done to serve and glorify you."

God pushes down his hands a second time and says, "Stop. You're not doing yourself any favors here. Why don't you go home and have a drink or something? Clear your head. You don't have things straight. In fact, you're worse off than that other pastor down the road who's been beating his chest in shame. In fact, he's too ashamed to even look at me when he prays. He can't stop confessing his sins to me."

But does that make any sense to us? No, it does not. How can the one pastor we would all praise and seek to imitate be worse off than the rotten pastor? How can a righteous pastor be worse than one who is about as immoral, or at least as worthless as pastors come? Can we at least give the pastor credit for his devotion to be a good pastor?

If we do, we make the same fatal error as the Pharisee. The Pharisee looks at his obedience, his good works, and the rewards by which he measures his relation to God. The Pharisee figures these are enough to keep him in good with God for the rest of his life. He does not see himself in relation to eternity. He does not recognize that all his righteousness, all he brings to God in prayer, is about as valuable as a rotting heap of bloody tampons as far as God is concerned (Isaiah 64:6).

But if that does not hit close enough to home, take a more common example. Suppose that you are an even better person than the good pastor. Imagine that you are not tempted by any sin except arguing, and even that is something you have resolved to overcome with God's help. Are you so sure that in relation to eternity you can keep yourself from ever getting angry? Are you certain that you can resist ever starting an argument with someone, even with God's help? Can you live at peace with other people even though there are limitless opportunities to argue? Will you go before God day after day, week after week, and say to the Maker of all things, "I strayed a little bit this week, but I know with your help I can get back on track"? Do you really think that is what St. Paul meant by "running the race," and "fighting the good fight of faith"?

No, it is not. The point of Jesus' parable is that none of our goodness is good enough to pass a test like that. The brutal reality is that God is not about to take a risk on us being able to do it either. God is not going to let us take our mess of a life, as we try to hold on and control it, into eternity. He will take only the emptiness of our death in the power of Jesus' resurrection. As Robert Capon describes in his book on Jesus' parables, *Kingdom, Grace, Judgment: Paradox, Outrage, and Vindication in the Parables of Jesus,* Jesus condemns the Pharisee because that religious man takes a stand on a life God cannot use. God commends the rotten tax collector because that man rests his case on a death God can use. The tax collector is a deadbeat. He is dead tired. He is dead in sin.

The Pharisee and tax collector and the good and rotten pastors are both dead in sin of course. But so long as the good pastor refuses to confess that he is dead in sin, he will be unable to believe and confess the truth about himself. He is so busy with spiritual bookkeeping, accounting for every good work and bad choice, he does not even notice that in Christ, God has torn up his ledger. All the good pastor's entries have been buried in a tomb about a twenty-minute walk from downtown Jerusalem.

But what about the rotten pastor? He goes home justified. Why? Because he confessed that all he had to offer God was his rottenness. All he has to bring before God is his sin and death. He does not have an impressive list of good works in his pocket. He does not have a well thought out plan to reform his rotten life. He has no vision for getting right with God. He comes before God with nothing that we might call "good." He comes into God's presence with nothing that puts religious types at ease. There is nothing about him that says to us, "This is why God justified him." Jesus does this in the parable so that all we are left with is the tax collector's sin and death and God's love for rotten sinners.

That is why, deep down, we hate this parable and all Jesus' parables. Jesus used parables to reveal the nightmare truth about each of us. We are afraid to celebrate the rotten pastor's justification because we know people who are just like him. We are just like him. There is no one who is left out of Jesus' parable, whether we are on team Pharisee or team tax collector.

That is the point of Jesus' parable. We are not the good pastor or the rotten pastor. We are not the Pharisee or the tax collector. We are both of them at the same time. The only difference between them is, as Jesus says, the one said, "Thank you, God, that I'm not like him . . ." The other, too ashamed to look up, beat his chest and said, "Forgive me, Lord. I am *the* sinner."

Jesus came to save sinners, of which each one of us may accurately say, "I am the worst." Each of us is *the* sinner. But this is not a sad confession. It is praise for a God who died for deadbeats like us—a Savior who was raised from the dead for we who are dead in sin. This is our comfort and one certainty in life and in death, today and always. In Jesus' death and resurrection, the books are closed. Our accounts with God are settled by Jesus' innocent suffering and death. There's nothing left for us to count up good or bad, nice or nasty, happy or miserable, living or dead. In Jesus, we are made the righteousness of God. All that we need to do to get right with God has already been done for us by Jesus.

Christianity is not about our belief in God. It is not about being nice or good. It is not about our traditions, rituals, and dogmas. It is all about Jesus. Christianity is, top to bottom, about what Jesus does for us. It is about God being God for us in the way of faithful, loving-kindness. It is about God being God for us in the way of grace and truth.

This reality has driven many, many people into the ditch opposite of moralistic, therapeutic deism. It started about two hundred years ago with theologians who got fed up with the old, pre-modern Reformation teaching that we are saved by grace alone, through faith alone, in Christ Jesus alone. It was not so much Jesus they had a problem with, though. It was the confession that Jesus died for sin and was raised for our justification. At the heart of the church's confession about Jesus, there is a message about God's judgment. If Jesus died to forgive sin, then we must have sin that needs forgiving. If we have sin that needs forgiving, and Jesus is the sole source of that forgiveness, then anyone not in Christ, as the apostle Paul says, is not forgiven. But what about people in the Amazon rainforests who have never heard the gospel? What about babies who die before they can be baptized? What about just plain old evil? Would Hitler get into heaven if he believed that Jesus died for his sin? The God who justifies the godless, it seems, was too untamed, immoral, and unfair for the theologians of the nineteenth century.

What those theologians did was not new. It has been our old Adam's project since the fall. But what was new was how their thoughts found their way into pop culture and have remained ever since. Instead of going out to discover what the Creator is doing in and for his creation, modern theologians of every stripe have fallen victim to the temptation to use God as an excuse to discover themselves. Since the Enlightenment, Christians in general have been more concerned about self-reinvention, about creating themselves from the inside out through their own works, than in paying attention to the fact that their true, eternal identity is already, and only, established for them by their relation to Jesus.

The ultimate victim of this move of theodicy—our attempt to explain why a perfectly good, almighty, and all-knowing God permits evil—has been God's Word. Instead of presenting an unsolvable theodicy, God's word often speaks in forensic language. God the Father sits in his Judge's seat, gavel in hand, listening to the facts of the case before him. Satan stands as the prosecuting attorney, who seeks a guilty conviction. The Holy Spirit, the Paraclete, plays the defense attorney. We sit in the defendant's seat.

Once the facts are presented in total by the prosecuting attorney, the Judge has no other option than to pronounce a guilty verdict. We have sinned against heaven and earth. It is an open-and-shut case. The Holy Spirit never once objects to any of Satan's assertions. And in the end, Satan does not even need to make a persuasive closing argument. Our guilt is irrefutable, and God's judgment is a sentence of death.

The gavel is about to fall when the Paraclete stands up and says, "One moment, Judge! The defense has not had a chance to call our star witness, Jesus the Christ." The Judge lowers his gavel and calls the witness to the stand, despite the prosecution's objections. Jesus approaches the stand, says, "Hi, Dad," swears by himself, and sits down. The prosecution approaches Jesus. "What could you possibly have to add that could change the verdict of this trial?" Jesus smiles and says, "I did it. I am the real culprit." Jesus then turns to the Judge, and says, "Whatever verdict you rendered, I gladly and willingly accept it on their behalf. Execute me in their place so that they may walk out of this courtroom declared not guilty on all counts." Satan screams. The Holy Spirit leans back in his chair and folds his arms. The Judge bangs his gavel. Jesus is escorted out of the courtroom by guards. Then the Judge turns to us and says, "You are free to go."

We are declared "not guilty" in Jesus' death for us. Everyone at all times and in all places is declared forgiven by the witness of Jesus' bloody suffering and death for us. This means people who do not deserve forgiveness are declared forgiven. To the religious and the critic, it seems that Jesus' forgiveness gets people off the hook. They want to at least participate in our justification. There has got to be something we must do to be saved. So, even if God's Word will not allow us to work out our own salvation, we simply change the story. The result is that God is unseated as Judge. Instead we relegate him to our defendant's chair and pull out all of our theodicy tricks. We take our place in the Judge's seat, pick up the gavel, and say, "All right! Now you, God, justify your actions to us." In this way, we sit in judgment of God. We decide what is acceptable and unacceptable behavior for God. We determine by our judgments whether someone deserves to be let off the hook for his or her crimes. When we give in to the temptation to judge God's actions, what we are really doing is trying to stand in God's place. We just cannot help ourselves. We are natural-born lawyers, but no matter how attractive our arguments may sound, they ultimately undermine God's authority.

An example of this is when a lawyer tested Jesus (Luke 10:25–37). The lawyer believed he had the perfect legal argument to prove Jesus was an irreligious, immoral charlatan. The lawyer believed in God. He knew the Ten Commandments. He was a patriot, who paid his taxes on time. He was a helpful neighbor and a valuable part of the community. His wisdom in matters of law was sought after by everyone, even the religious leaders. So, the religious leaders thought, who better to pin Jesus down once and for all?

The lawyer, like us, lived in a world of what is earned and what is deserved. He lived in a world of just deserts—a world where people exist by what they earn, what they owe, and what they have got coming to them. For a lawyer, life is about rewards, punishments, and credits. It is a life spent keeping track of people's performances, accomplishments, and achievements. Do well, and we will be treated well. Do bad, and we get the bad in spades. For a lawyer, everyone gets what they deserve. But it is not just lawyers who live this way. We are all born into this. We old Adam sinners are all lawyers at heart. That is why we imagine that we can do something to earn absolution, forgiveness, or eternal life.

That is the way it goes for all lawyers, especially those who are doggedly religious. That is why the lawyer asked Jesus the question: "Hey, Jesus, since you think you're so smart: 'What must I *do* to inherit eternal life?'" He did not ask, "What must I do to solve my neighbor's hunger and poverty?" He did not ask, "What must I do to save my family from pain and hurt?" When a major eternal life or death problem needs an answer there is no time to quibble about such minor problems when a major problem needs an answer.

It is the ultimate problem for all of us that forms the subtext of all our religious pursuits. There is nothing bigger than eternal life. But like us, the lawyer believed that eternal life hung on what he must *do*. That is why he asked Jesus, "What must I *do* to inherit eternal life?" But Jesus didn't answer the question. Instead, he asked the lawyer a question. "So, you want to *do* something to get eternal life? Okay, what do the Ten Commandments say you must do?" The lawyer said, "That's easy. Even a child knows the answer. Love God with all that you've got. Love your neighbor as you love yourselves. Follow the Golden Rule. Simple. Now tell me what to do. Give me a real-life application sermon for once!" "All right," Jesus said. "Don't wait for me to point you in the right direction. Go right ahead and do the commandments. Give it a shot. But I'm warning you, you must love God and your neighbor perfectly. Otherwise your eternal life is in some serious jeopardy." "Who is my neighbor," the lawyer asked. "If my eternal life hangs on this, I've got to know, who is my neighbor? Define 'neighbor.'"

So Jesus told this parable: "Your neighbor is every broken-down person who crosses your path. If you want to be sure that eternal life is yours, love God and love your neighbor as yourself. As long as you help *everyone* in need, like the Samaritan, regardless of cost or convenience—as long as you love God with your *entire* being and *complete* strength—salvation is yours. Every time you are on the highway and see a stranded motorist with his hood up or a scruffy-looking hitchhiker, you have got to stop and help."

We ask Jesus our law questions, and he gives us his word of law answer. Then, once he blows up all our legal arguments, he finishes us off with a gospel parable. We are left with only two options now: try to engage the law answer with more legal wrangling or accept the gospel parable as a gracious gift. Left to ourselves, like the lawyer, we always choose the law way. That is why we prefer God-talk to Jesus' words. We savor the sweet nothings of our words, because they are more appealing to us than God's Word. And rather than sit passive while Jesus works out our salvation, we go to work to explain away God's judgment against sin, death, and damnation. This is who we end up sitting in judgment of God or accepting an impotent, neutered God who just wants us to be happy.

As he did with the lawyer, Jesus snuffs out all our religious aspirations. He sends us a preacher to announce the truth: forgiveness, life, and salvation hangs on Jesus alone. Eternal life hangs on his perfect life for us. He was beaten to a bloody pulp for us. He was strung up between rebels for us. He was left for dead on the cross for us. All this he did for us, even though the guilt for his murder falls on all of us. He loves us there on the cross. On the cross, God provides us with a love that we do not deserve and have not earned It is a gift. It is free for us because Jesus did all the work for us. It is forgiveness, life, and eternal salvation worked out for us by pure grace for Christ's sake because there, at Golgotha, arms open wide, Jesus holds us all in his incredible love.

We are completely passive, and he is totally active. That is what offends us more than anything about what the Bible has to say about Jesus. There is nothing we hate more than passivity, especially in relation to something as important as eternal life. We must have time and choices. We must have the freedom to work out our salvation. But the gospels teach us the exact opposite. Unlike other religions, which attempt to explain God and belief by way of legal arguments and what we must do to be saved, the Bible sets up Jesus as a categorical rejection of all such religious arguments.

Jesus says about himself, "I am the Way, the Truth, and the Life." He alone is the way to salvation. The promised grace of God comes through Jesus, not by what we do or leave undone. Whatever is not Jesus is not the way to salvation. No matter how invested we are in working out our salvation, if the way in which it occurs is not Jesus then we are always in error. Likewise, whatever we may believe is true about God and ourselves, if the truth is not Jesus alone then we have not located the truth. We are caught in a lie. We are not running toward God; we are running away from him, deeper into error, untruth, and death.

Jesus does not come to offer a recipe for how to repair our mess of a life. He does not show us how to get our life together. The only message Jesus gives to his church is that grace alone saves, through faith in him. It is not a religious message as such because it does not point us back to our doing. Look into any religion and we quickly discover a set of doctrines that govern our thoughts, words, and behavior. We love these formulas. In a way, we crave religious dogma over freedom in Christ Jesus.

This is why Jesus is not someone we desire or wish for, not according to any earthly measure. It offends us that he does not demand that we straighten up and fly right. Like the religious leaders in the gospels, it angers us that his presence simply confronts us with the undeniable facts: we want a plan, a method, a scheme, or a recipe that enables us to become the agents of our own salvation. But he refuses to provide one. Instead, we are told that God "chose us in him before the foundation of the world to be holy and blameless in his presence. In love he predestined us for adoption as his sons through Jesus Christ, according to the purpose of his will" (Ephesians 1:4–5).

God's good pleasure, not our choice, saves us from sin and death. Any question about how we ought to react to this good news, or how we should behave as a consequence, only serves to turn us away from Jesus as the source of God's good pleasure. When we turn our back to the cross, we legislate God's Word. We institutionalize Jesus' relationship with his people. We establish hierarchies with Jesus at the top, and when those fail us, we turn around and sell Jesus as the friend of sinners. Whatever we need to do to regulate God's relation to us, to keep him at a distance so we can retain personal agency, we will do it. Whatever it takes to break free from having to sit passive while Jesus hogs all the glory, we will do it in the name of thanking, praising, and serving God.

Thankfully, God is not the least bit preoccupied with our attempts to save institutions, our organizations, legal wrangling, or ourselves. Jesus comes to save sinners, not as an ideal to be reached but as an actual fact in the present tense. He comes through his words of promise and gifts to justify the ungodly. That is the foundation and lifeblood of Jesus' people. He is the Son of God, who comes to us whether we like it or not, are ready for him or not, or think we deserve it or not.

Everyone is eligible for the gospel of Jesus Christ because everyone is godless. Even after conversion, the old Adam in us continues to struggle with this new reality. If everyone is invited to the wedding feast of the Lamb in his kingdom, we reason, what is to keep the wrong people out of our religious gatherings? Answer: nothing. Everyone and anything that previously cut us off from God's grace and peace in Christ is left for dead in his tomb.

The only criteria for a right relation to God is whether we receive as a gift that all of life and salvation are out of our control, and they always have been. Jesus alone comes to us when we were still enemies of God, suffers only to be rejected by us, even allows us to execute him, and still rises from death to rescue us from all that drives us to become religious people. God's uncompromising yes in Jesus sets us free from all such worry about our choices and worthiness so that we can live a new life in relation to Christ Jesus. We are freed by God's Word and gifts.

Freed from what? Jesus sets us free from religion, through the forgiveness of sin so that we can live, trusting that God has already prepared our good works for us before the foundation of the world. We are free to love our neighbors as he first loved us, with a selfless, self-giving love that cost him his life.

What, then, is God's law to a Christian? We get in trouble when we treat the Ten Commandments and God's law generally like a do-it-yourselves salvation project. We ignore what the Law teaches us about ourselves: "All have sinned and come short of the glory of God." And, "there is no one that does good, no, not one." And, "against you, you only, have I sinned" (Romans 3:10–12; Psalm 14:1–3, 53:1–3). The Law humbles us, causes us to repent, and shows us the truth about ourselves. We are shown that we are worse than we imagined, that we are all "sold under sin." God's Word of Law drives us to ask, "Who will help me?" When that question is forced out of us, then we are ready for the gospel. We are ready to hear that there is no way for us to help ourselves, or expect help from God, outside of Christ crucified for us.

Jesus is not for us in the way of other gods, as Judge or Executioner. He is the Lamb of God whose blood is shed for the sin of the world. God holds not a single sin against us for Christ's sake. Jesus' blood covers all sin. This is why we receive grace and forgiveness from God. This is why God sends a preacher to declare us righteous for Christ's sake. This is why we are Christians. It is why Martin Luther said during his Galatians lectures in 1535:

> We define a Christian as follows: A Christian is not someone who has no sin or feels no sin; he is someone to whom God does not impute his sin. This doctrine brings form consolation to troubled consciences amid genuine terrors. It is not in vain, therefore, that so often and so diligently we inculcate the doctrine of the forgiveness of sins and of the imputation of righteousness for the sake of Christ, as well as the doctrine that a Christian does not have anything to do with the Law and sin, especially in a time of temptation. For, to the extent that he is a Christian he is above the Law and sin, because in his heart he has Christ, the Lord of the Law, as a ring has a gem . . . Therefore, a Christian, properly defined, is free of all laws and is subject to nothing, internally or externally (LW 25:133–34).

Rather than build a religious following around the teachings of Jesus, as if he were just another guru, the church proclaims his death and resurrection for the forgiveness of sin. It is the same forgiveness, as Luther says, that sets us free from the Law and sin so long as our hearts are in Christ through faith. This is what sets us free to call ourselves Christian without doubt or reservation. We live in the power of Jesus' resurrection, in the forgiveness of sin, in relation to God and each other.

The good news of Christ Jesus is that in the power of his death and resurrection, this man who is God has freed us from worry about whether we are getting our religious ducks in a row. Now we walk in forgiveness, free to love God and each other without a recipe, a playbook, or an accountant's ledger. On account of Jesus, the books are closed, and there is nothing for us to do except enjoy the wonderful, amazing, gracious gift of forgiveness, life, and salvation he declares to us through a preacher. In the end, no matter how it is dressed up and made palatable to us, religion teaches us to "do more, better." But on the cross, Jesus declares, "It is done."

I used to believe, when I first began to read C.S. Lewis and Augustine, at the orphanage, and during those lunches with my pastor, that my salvation depended on what I believed about God, my worship on Sunday morning, and my actions during the week. But, all along it was never about what I do or do not do for God. It is all about what Jesus does for me. He dies for me. He defeats Satan for me. Faith, hope, and love are what he creates in me through his gospel promise of forgiveness, his baptismal grace, and strengthening faith and increasing love through the consumption of his body and blood in the Lord's Supper. It was never about me. It was and is and always will be about what he does to save me and all sinners in his bloody suffering and death at Golgotha.

CHAPTER 5

I BELIEVE IN GOD, NOW WHAT DO I DO?

What do you do when you believe in God? How do you act upon that belief? For me, it was to seek out other believers. And since I had zeroed in on Christianity, that meant I had to seek out a church. I attended high mass on Good Friday at a Roman Catholic cathedral. The Latin, copious use of incense, and gold-embroidered vestments were a distraction for me. I could not understand what was said. I could not see very well, since the incense set off my allergies. The gold-embroidered vestments seemed to advertise something about this church that was in contradiction to the Bible's teaching that we are to "humble ourselves before the Lord" (James 4:10).

The actions of the priests, and the worshipers, all appeared to me to be so much theater. The priest would chant, raise his hands, bow, turn toward the altar, genuflect, and so on. The people would stand up, sit down, kneel, stand up, chant, bow their heads in prayer, and make the sign of the cross over and over again. What was all this about, I wondered. *Do they all know Latin? Why are we doing this? How does everyone seem to know what happens next except for me? What purpose does any of this serve in relation to God?* The whole experience left me frustrated and anxious. I thought, *maybe I do not belong in this church. Maybe the problem is me. I don't know the language. I don't understand what to do. Time to move on and look for another church.*

The next worship I participated in was at a suburban Lutheran church. Instead of chants, incense, and gold-embroidered vestments, this church had a pastor dressed in a simple white robe with what looked like a green table runner draped around his neck. He wore a simple pectoral cross. The band, situated stage right, was enthusiastic, if out of tune and sometimes struggling to find the beat. The projection screen above the altar displayed the words of the songs, readings, and order of worship. It was a laid-back experience. Everybody seemed so happy. At the time, I remember thinking, *I've never seen so many people smiling this much this early in the morning. This is creepy!*

But unlike my experience following the mass, after worship at this congregation, numerous people introduced themselves to me. They shook my hand. One old lady hugged me. It was disturbing for me since I had never been treated like this by strangers. I did not even get a moment to myself to enjoy the bad coffee they served. Lutherans were in my face, smiling their toothy smiles, grabbing at me. As we drove away, I said to the friend who had attended worship with me, "They seem so desperate, and that worship service came off as bad karaoke."

This was to become a recurring theme in my early attempts to engage in worship with other believers. Whether it was Roman, Lutheran, Baptist, Presbyterian, Episcopalian, Methodist, or nondenominational, I was either given a cold shoulder or smothered with attention. The priest, pastor, or minister either disappeared through a side door after worship or sat with me to sell me on the reasons I should join that church.

After two years, I concluded that Christianity was a lot of people doing a lot of different things to worship God. But with the variations in worship forms and styles, and the way they went about worship, I wondered which group got it right. Was there such a thing as worship done right? Just as I had tried to gather data on what different religions believed about God, now

I was faced with a similar problem. Is there anything uniquely Christian about Christian worship in comparison to way other religions worshipped? Also, what was the reason for gathering together to worship? To get at this, I went back to my books. I also asked more questions of family, friends, and acquaintances. What did their religion understand by the term *worship*? What do we hope to get out of worshiping God? Do we even have to worship God? If God is everywhere, then why do I have to go to that building down the street and give them money if I want to get in good with my Creator? Why does God need my money? These were the sorts of questions I asked, and I wanted answers.

These questions were actually a cover for my true intent. What I was really after was an answer to a deeper question—a question that had tormented me for years even before I believed in God. Could an addict like me be saved from addiction and the hellish ruin I had made of my life?

The question that drove me to examine life, the universe, and everything was rooted in addiction. Stronger than my new-found belief in God was the conviction that I was enslaved to alcohol and drugs. I could not get free of them. Nothing and nobody were able to help me. I followed the same path as my father and his father and probably his father's father. The words of St. Paul, when I first read them, were all too real to me: "who will deliver me from this body of death?" (Romans 7:24) This was at the root of all my questions about worship. Can worshiping God set me free from addiction and a pathetic death? Can someone as unworthy of God's attention as I get relief? Does God actually love me, and if so where do I go to receive God's love in a concrete, real way?

I had many questions. At the bottom of them all was my need to escape addiction. I knew I had reached a sort of terminal velocity. I recognized that alcohol and drugs had overtaken me. Every day, my every thought and action served the goal of getting drunk and stoned. I used family, friends, and coworkers to feed my habit. If someone did not or could not support my addiction, I cut them off, accusing them of betraying me for one cooked reason or another. What I did not realize at the time, even though I recognized my dependency, was that alcohol and drugs had become my gods.

I trusted and loved what alcohol and drugs could do for me more than I trusted anybody or anything. I feared losing them more than I feared breaking up with a girlfriend, begin estranged from my family, or getting fired from a job. For more than ten years I was captivated by alcohol and drugs, because unlike family, friends, and work they were consistent. They were dependable. They never let me down, because they always delivered on their promise to anesthetize the pain—pain that was a manifestation of shame, fear, guilt, and blame that originated in large part from what had happened in our home when I was a boy.

I grew up with an abusive addict. All the men on my father's side of the family were abusive drunks. I watched my father and his brothers sabotage relationships, jobs, and happiness time and again because of alcohol and drugs. Sadly, I grew up to ape their behavior. I think this was also a significant factor in my rejection of God. First, I rejected God because of the abuse I suffered. Second, I rejected God because of what I experienced growing up in an ecosystem of addiction. Third, I rejected God because I did not have room in my life for another god. Alcohol and drugs were gods that demanded all my time, attention, and energy.

From as early as I can remember, alcohol and drugs were a normal part of our family's activities. Alcohol and drugs framed every holiday, birthday, and family gathering. They were just always there. When we celebrated, people were drunk and high. When we fought, mourned, or made up, alcohol and drugs were the stimulus.

When I went to seek out worship experiences, I was on the hunt for relief. I wanted to shift the spotlight from alcohol and drugs onto God. More specifically, I wanted to know how Jesus was going to rescue me from addiction. But the more churches I went into, the more churches I walked out of frustrated and enraged. I remember one sermon in particular. In the midst of his sermon, a cheery, well-groomed pastor said, "God loves you just the way you are!" Although that was as blunt as I had heard it put, I listened to many, many sermons that expressed the same sentiment: "God loves you just the way you are. Now go out there and live a life that will cause God to smile down upon you!" As a drug addict, this sentiment did not give me comfort. It did not free me from fear and anxiety. It condemned me. To be blunt, the gravity of those words was so massive that, at the time, I used it as another justification to attempt suicide by overdose.

This was not the godly love that led Jesus to bleed out and die for the sin of the world. What was unique about a therapeutic message that announces, "God loves you just the way you are"? Why did the pastor not understand that for those who cling to hope like a drowning man clings to a piece of debris, such a message was hopeless? I wonder, were they ever regularly engaged with the kind of questions that I asked or that get asked by the people I minister to today? When I asked questions, they were often met with caring but blank stares. This was especially true when I brought up my addiction. It seemed at the time, and unfortunately persists still in my conversations, that when I bring up the relation of worship to addiction, most people cannot make the connection.

As an addict, belief and the way it is expressed through worship is not a matter of taste. It is not one more thing on my calendar that I need to check off before a new week begins. Worship is not "my God time." What God we believe in and confess matters. How we express that in our worship is of utmost importance. Because, whether we recognize it or not, belief as it is expressed in the church's worship is a very concrete, real matter of life and death. But in my experience, where I struggled is where many people struggle, especially those who stand in the breach between unbelief and trust, hopelessness and comfort. Worship is not us acting out ancient rituals to earn God's attention or celebrating life with our God. Worship is theology. It is a confession of faith formed in the breach between doubt and belief, condemnation and relief, death and new life.

Theology is how we explain our experience of God. St. Augustine defined it as "reasoning or discussion concerning the Deity."[3] When we engage in theological discussion, we are confessing to each other and to the world how we understand our relation to God, what kind of a person God is for us, and what he does for us. Theology expresses how and why we praise, describe, and talk about God. We "do theology," so to speak, so we and other people can know God. Worship is not just about the music, the message, or the theater of it all. Worship is repeated Sunday after Sunday, month after month, and year after year so that that theological repetition shapes our faith more than most Christians realize.

What I have encountered since walking into my first worship experience, though, is that Christians appear to be more concerned about how worship affects our mood. For this reason, we often get caught up using worship as a cover to express our impulses—what we must do and what we ought to think and say in worship—rather than focusing our attention on who is doing the doing. Is worship the time we have agreed upon when we gather to offer our sacrifices of praise and thanks to God? Is worship our action? I believe the Bible and experience prove that when worship is primarily about our actions, it is no different than any other religion's worship.

If we treat worship as a celebration of life with God, for example, then our actions in worship seem to be futile, for God does not seem to be paying attention to us. But what if worship is not about what we do to get God's attention? What if worship is God's action for us where God makes himself available to us in a very specific way? This is the difference between worship as our sacrifice, a transaction between God and us, and worship as God serving us with his gifts. I think this is the primary way we ought

---

[3] Augustine, *City of God*, Book VIII. i.

to distinguish Christian worship from all other kinds of worship. What makes Christian worship unique is the trajectory of the worship.

Worship is not the movement of us to God. It is the movement of God in and upon us. In the biblical sense, God promises to provide the gift for our worship and to be the gift for our worship. He promises to be the Giver and the gift. That, in a nutshell, is whom Jesus chooses to be for us: the Lamb of God sacrificed for our sins and the sins of the world. This radical translation of reality is what I yearned for all those years bouncing from church to church. It is what I hunted for in every worship experience. I did not so much care about the music, the sermon, or what I thought must or ought to be the way Christians worship God. All I cared about was (and all I still care about is) where is Jesus as Giver and gift for me? Where is the blood of the Lamb that sets me free from my captivation to addiction to be a child of God?

I did not need to be set free in a metaphorical sense. I did not need an intellectual or spiritual lift from worship. All I wanted was to be set free from addiction, which is just a shorthand confession for, "I need to be set free from the very real manifestations of sin and death that threaten to destroy my life here and now, and for eternity."

For someone who came late into the faith, who did not want a lot of generic God talk or feel-good worship, I wanted Jesus and Jesus only. I wanted to receive that measureless, unlimited love that compelled him to take my sin and death upon himself. I did not need to hear, "God loves you just the way you are!" I did not want to hear, "Live a life worthy of God's attention." I did not even want to hear, "Go in peace, to serve the Lord." Admonition and exhortation could not compete against the addiction that always whispered to me to go back to the safety and comfort of my gods, alcohol, and drugs.

If worship was primarily about my effort to earn God's attention, to get in good with the Almighty, then I was sunk. There was nothing about me that I could hold up before God to say, "Here is the best I have to offer." The "best" I could offer was that I believed I was garbage, a mistake, or a doomed addict who had used up all his tomorrows.

The more time I spent with Christians at worship, the more I noticed that the spotlight was pointed at me, my intentions, motives, or, worse, the thoughts and feelings of my heart. When God or Jesus were mentioned I seemed to be treated as more of a passive observer than an active participant. We made our beginning in the name of the Lord. We offered God our prayers of praise and thanksgiving. We offered back to God what he first gave us—our time, money, and possessions, which were said to be signs of his great love for us—but I always wondered why God needed our time when he is always with us? He is the beginning and the end. He is the One in whom we live, move, and have our being. Why does the Creator of more than 140 billion galaxies need my money and possessions, especially since he gave them to me? Why does God love a re-gifter? I had a lot of questions. I probably annoyed a lot of pastors, but at root the questions were all about one thing: is worship about my actions or God's actions? Is it my sacrifices or God's promises that make worship uniquely Christian? I still believe this is the difference between true and false worship. Also, it is the difference between our worship of a God who satisfies the yes and no of our personal tastes and the Christ who comes as Giver and gift regardless of what we imagine God can and must do for us.

Jesus came to save sinners. Before Jesus on the cross we are *the* sinner he came to save. This is not a sad confession. This is not something intended to shame or embarrass us. This is not something to mumble about under our breath. It is a confession that praises the God who seeks and saves the lost. He strengthens the weak. He died for us deadbeats. It is a confession that praises the Savior who was raised from the dead for us who are dead in sin. This is a confession that offers comfort and certainty in life and in death, today and always.

In the parable of the Pharisee and the tax collector, Jesus says that when we enter into his house the books are closed. There is nothing left to count up, good or bad. If we think it is the right thing to do to come before God to worship him on account of our goodness or to put on a good, we are dead wrong. But in Christ, we are declared forgiven, freed from sin and death to worship the One who rescues us from the messes we have made, our ill-conceived plans for our life, and our doomed attempts to save ourselves. In Christian worship we believe the promise. We receive God's cross-wise promise that declares: "You are *the* sinner who goes home justified."

When Christian worship becomes just another flavor of that old-time religion, it is primarily about us, our good intentions, our pious attitude, and what we must do to earn God's favor. But when it is tuned up to the confession that Jesus, our God and Lord, "was handed over to death for our trespasses and was raised for our justification" (Romans 4:25), we are on to something truly remarkable. That God died for us and was raised from death for our justification is something unheard of in all other forms of religious and secular worship. Christian worship is not about what we do or say to God to get his attention. Neither is it about receiving our well-deserved reward. Christian worship is nothing more or less than Jesus himself speaking to us through his Word that we respond to through prayer, praise, and thanksgiving. Anything added to or taken away from this simple maxim threatens to derail Christian worship and turn it back into just another transaction we negotiate with God.

Christian worship hangs on God's Word. If God does not speak to us, how can we know whether God is for us? Since we cannot know God as God for us unless he reveals himself to us in the way of Jesus, how can we then pray to him, praise him, and thank him for all he does for us if he does not initiate the action on our behalf? What God says to us is of the greatest importance. Does he speak a word of judgment or grace? Does he convict us with his Word of Law, or does he absolve us with his word of gospel?

When God sends a preacher to speak his word of law to us, we are convicted of sin. The law says, "Thou shall, and thou shall not." "Do this and you will live; don't do this and you will die." In this way, we sinners hear the word of law as a warning: "You better get your act together. Straighten up and fly right, or God's judgment will fall upon you!" We hear God's word of law as an exhortation to act. Obey God or perish. We hear God's word of law as a call to obedience. We imagine that "You shall" and "You shall not" are appeals to our unwillingness to follow God's commandments. We extrapolate from this that we must then have some amount of free will to do what God commands. "God would not command the impossible," we argue, "because if he were to command something that is impossible for us to do well, that would make him a rather arbitrary and capricious deity, and his judgment would therefore be very unjust."

This attitude goes all the way back to Eden and the invention of religion. When Adam and Eve ate the fruit and their eyes were opened, they were like God. They knew good and evil. But they were not gods. As a result, even though they could distinguish good from evil, they were powerless to do anything about it. They could recognize good and evil, but they were impotent to effect any real change one way or the other. They knew good and evil, but they were exposed, vulnerable, and suddenly aware of their limitations. And in their self-awareness, having rebelled against God's Word, they attempted to save themselves at the expense of the other. This is the essence of all religious worship. First, we recognize that because we have rebelled against God, we are vulnerable and exposed. We are at the mercy of forces outside our control. Worse yet, we are at the mercy of the very One we betrayed. Second, since we are guilty of rebellion against our Creator, he has promised that the consequence for our action is death. Third, we throw someone or something at God's imminent judgment in the hope that he will accept our sacrifice and spare us from death. Last, we give thanks that we are spared God's furious anger and judgment until the next time we rebel and must repeat the steps all over again—day after day, week after week—until our life is thrown onto the sacrificial altar.

When God's word of law convicts us of sin, we scatter. We run every which way to try to find someone or something we can throw at the mess we have made of our life. We search for a fit sacrifice that can take our place in the judgment. But no matter what we put before God, it is never enough. God's anger toward sin can never be satisfied by our efforts. The endless number of religions we have invented that are all founded on the premise that to earn paradise and avoid damnation we must offer a sacrifice to our God all but proves this.

But what if God does not speak his word of law to us to appeal to our willingness to obey him? What if God commands the impossible on purpose? Then, the purpose and goal of his word of law would be to keep us from trying to satisfy a judgment against sin that can never be exhausted. This would mean, in effect, that the purpose for all religions would be nullified. If God does not require our sacrifices to satisfy his judgment against sin, then this would mean that God commands the impossible so that we stop, turn to him, and confess, "Lord, I cannot by my own reason or strength come to you. Despite all my efforts to change the outcome, all my sacrifices leave me feeling more uncertain and anxious. I am powerless to change my damnable destiny. But if you choose, you can have mercy on me."

God speaks his word of law to us, and we imagine he then expects us to act. Our action then forms the basis for a transactional view of our relation to God, a tit-for-tat kind of relationship. God speaks. We act to obey his commands. He rewards our efforts. Our sacrifice then becomes the way in which we interact with deity. God is impassive and impersonal, and he waits for us to come to him. If we do not come in the proper way at the right time with the correct words and offerings, then he will rouse himself and come to us in judgment. But when God comes to collect, who will pick up the tab?

And God's Son? What of him? How does he factor into this? In the transactional way we imagine worship, Jesus sacrifices himself to open the way for us to obey God's commands. What could not be done before, Christians can now accomplish because Jesus revealed to us through his living and dying as the Lamb of God how to obey the law. Jesus becomes our example of godly obedience and sacrifice. Unfortunately, even though it invokes Jesus' name, there is nothing uniquely Christian about this kind of worship.

What makes Christian worship "Christian" is Jesus the Christ. This may seem like a no-brainer, but when Jesus is dangled in front of us as an example of godly obedience and sacrifice, we are left in the proverbial lurch. Since "the law came in to increase the trespass" (Romans 5:20), our obedience to the law only results in an increase of sin. Even if we cannot do what God commands without increasing sin, at least we can love God's word of law and hate the fact that we continue to sin, right? Yes we can, Paul says in Romans 7:14–25, but we are still not spared judgment on that account. We still must die. That is why for me, all these years later, I still view worship as a matter of life and death.

Rather than begin our talk about Christian worship with God's word of law, we begin with how God speaks to us through Jesus. That is, "Long ago, at many times and in many ways, God spoke to our fathers by the prophets, but in these last days he has spoken to us by his Son" (Hebrews 1:1–2). Our God is a God who speaks to his people. He is not an impersonal, dispassionate God who awaits our sacrifices. Instead, he comes to us, nearer to us than our next breath, to unleash a flood of grace upon us. He does this by way of his beloved Son, who we are directed to listen to. Jesus then gives us specific words for our worship that we can trust are true, God-pleasing words.

The way God expresses worship done right, done his way, is in the way of promise. God's Word present for us is the way of worship. If God's Word is not present, concrete, and real for us, then we have to wonder, "What is the point of worship?" From

God's side of the street, the correct direction of worship is from God down to us, not us up to God. God comes to us in his Word, the second person of the Trinity, the Son, Jesus the Christ. He is the One to whom God commands us to listen. God sends us a preacher for the same reason, to make himself present to us in his concrete, real Word. God desires to be incarnate among us. We sinners do not go to him with our sacrifices. He comes to us with a specific word of promise, the Lamb of God, the one-time-for-all-time sacrifice for all our sin.

God's promise is Jesus. He is God in the flesh. He is concrete and real. Jesus has a birthday, a death day, and a resurrection day. He is our God. He is not a slave to time and space, but he chose to bind himself to us at a certain time in a certain place for our benefit. All of Christian worship confesses and points to Jesus alone. In this way all of Christian worship is grounded in the language of promise and gift. Jesus comes as giver and gift. He gives himself to us in words, water, bread, and wine. We do not have to climb up to him. We do not have to try to figure out what God expects from us. We do not have to work ourselves up to the right level of sincerity, purity, and readiness. We do not have to go in search of words to describe God. We have received a clear word from God, that Jesus was crucified for the sin of the world. Jesus died for our sin and was raised for our justification. This is spoken to us as a promise that is trustworthy and true because it is not an idea in search of meaning. The promise is God's. Christian worship declares to the whole world that God is God for us in the person of Jesus. There is no need to go in search of God. He has been among us, speaking to us, the whole time.

What is to be done about this turn toward the self in worship? Simple. The gospel must be preached! That means we delete anything from our worship that moves us in the wrong direction. We cut out any sacrificial language that does not direct us to Jesus' Good Friday sacrifice for us. We expunge from worship any words that replace God's Word of promise with our works. It is not our sacrifice, our prayers of thanks and praise, or our symbols that make for God-pleasing worship. Just as the sixteenth-century reformers removed praying to the saints, the addition of all sorts of unhelpful symbols added onto baptism, and making the Lord's Supper a sacrifice, so too can we at present push back against traditions and rituals that bury Jesus and the public proclamation of his last will and testament.

Everything that happens in worship can be judged according to one standard: does this deliver Jesus as gift? Is Jesus present in concrete reality for us as our crucified and risen Lord? Is the good news about Jesus Christ preached in such a way that faith in Christ Jesus is renewed and love stirred up among Christians? Whatever traditions and rituals lead us in the wrong direction and oppose Jesus alone as the source and focus of worship must be cast out. The only thing that makes worship uniquely Christian is that Christ crucified for the sin of the world is preached, sung, and prayed in such a way that God is the One, and the only One, whom we acknowledge creates justifying faith and selfless, self-giving love in us through his Word. Then we can pray, praise, and give thanks to God for all his faithful, loving kindness toward us. We can rest in the confidence that our worship is done God's way, in a God-pleasing way, in the way of Jesus as giver and gift.

Christian worship is dependent on God's Word. In this way, worship is literally a matter of life and death. If God does not speak to us before, during, and after we enter into our churches, we will go looking for better, more spiritual, more religious words. Sooner than later we will turn in on ourselves to find the words we crave to hear. But God's first word to us cuts this off right away. He says, "You shall have no other gods before me" (Exodus 20:3). His second word to us provides a living, breathing option to our deathly pursuit of better gods and words. Martin Luther summed this creedal confession up best when he wrote:

I believe that Jesus Christ—true God, Son of the Father from eternity, and true man, born of the Virgin Mary—is my Lord. He has redeemed

*me, a lost and condemned creature, saved me at great cost from sin,
death and the power of the devil—not with silver or gold, but with his
holy and precious blood and his innocent suffering and death. (Small
Catechism, The Creed, Second Article)*

God speaks his word of law to us: "I am your God, so knock it
off with all your chasing after people and things that are not
me." Second, God speaks his word of gospel to us: "You can give
up on being your own savior. Jesus is your Savior. He died for
your sin and rose for your justification. All this is declared and
bequeathed to you for free. Believe it. Receive it."

God's Word is where Christian worship begins and ends. But
it is a specific word from God. It is God's Word. The direction is
from God to us. It is all from God to us in the way of promise
and gift. We do not need to go looking for better, more spiritual,
more religious words. We hear the published Word of God read
to us. We listen to a preacher announce the good news about
Jesus Christ for us. We are baptized in Jesus' name. We receive
the bread and wine we confess are the body and blood of Jesus
given and shed for us for the forgiveness of sin. All of Christian
worship is bent toward this one object—that is, God's word in
Christ Jesus where God himself gives forgiveness, life, and salvation. He is the object of our worship because he alone is our
righteousness apart from works of the Law. All of Christian worship therefore takes on a singular focus: Christ Jesus coming to
us to forgive our sin.

Contrary to what we may believe, God does not help those
who help themselves. Instead, he gifts forgiveness, life, and
salvation to the poor in Spirit, the empty, the helpless, and the
ungodly with his Christ. Then, in response to his faithful, loving
kindness toward us, we confess that we neither deserve nor have
earned this amazing grace. Next, we thank him for all the good
he does for us, especially for forgiving us ungodly sinners. We
ask for more of his faithfulness and love to be directed toward
us. We say amen and go into our earthly vocations in peace and

joy. And when we make a mess of our vocations, as we always do, God gathers us to himself again to pronounce that on account of Jesus he no longer remembers our sin.

When Jesus is for us in the way of promise, in the way of gift, all of life is revealed to be worship. Whether one is a pastor, custodian, student, grandparent, soldier, or stockbroker, when we live in faith in Christ Jesus everything can be received as gift. Even our struggles and afflictions, suffering and crosses, can be received as gift because all of creation—even the afflictions that emerge from being a sinful creature—is bent toward our salvation.

A good example of this is found in the book of Jonah. God says to Jonah that Nineveh's evil is so great he cannot ignore it any longer. But rather than send his prophet to condemn Nineveh, God tells Jonah to go and justify the Ninevites. Jonah does not have any desire to go and preach to his enemies a word that flies in the face of human logic and justice. And yet, no matter which way Jonah goes to escape God's will, God bends all creation to the end that his preacher goes to the Ninevites to preach them into justification. This is why even the cows in Nineveh are made to repent in sackcloth and ashes. When the Word comes, he does not return to his Father empty-handed. Even cows are made to bow to the power of God's Word.

God sends us a preacher, whether we like it or not. This one is sent to us to announce, publicly, God's will for us in the way of Jesus crucified for the sin of the world. The preacher is sent to pronounce an absolution in Jesus' name. Likewise, the preacher is sent to deliver the gifts of God's Word in water, bread, and wine, which also serve to declare to us forgiveness, life, and salvation in Jesus' saving name. As he did for Nineveh, so he does for us at present. All of creation is an instrument through which our Savior works to redeem us.

God raises up preachers for us. He sends us a flesh-and-blood baptized sinner to call us to repent and believe. He sends us a sheep dog who chases us with God's Word into the sheep fold of

Jesus, our good shepherd. And so we do not cry foul when the preacher says something we do not want to hear, Jesus says, "The one who hears you hears me" (Luke 10:16).

This, of course, does not mean that anything out of a pastor or preacher's mouth is God's Word. There are ways to discern this. Does the preacher distinguish God's Word of law and gospel? Is the law preached in such a way that it is clear what is demanded of us in the commandments? What God condemns as sin? How he judges sin? Is God's Word of law held up as the most salutary doctrine of life that condemns sin, but likewise points to how Jesus perfectly kept the law for us? Is there an ultimate word that proclaims Jesus delivered to us, for us? Does the pastor announce new life for us from Jesus' death and resurrection? Is condemnation shut up by an absolute absolution that declares Christ Jesus dead and risen for sinners?

If we do not hear this straight and true from our preachers, we are not hearing God's Word. We hear words, and some of them may even sound remarkably similar to God's Word as it is published in the Bible. But unless it is God's Word of law and gospel, we cannot be sure that what we hear from our pastor is God's actual words intended for us. We need the "for-you-ness" of the gospel to be preached to us. Otherwise they may be words about Jesus, but they are not words that give Jesus to us.

The "for-you-ness" of the gospel is the thing. Luther highlighted this in his *Small Catechism* when he described the promises of God "for you" as the real good news. Without hyperbole or exaggeration, it is everything. Why? The difference between a proclamation and a description is the "for you" of the gospel. We can talk about Jesus. We can describe grace and forgiveness. But that does not give us Jesus in actual fact. When the words "given and shed for you for the forgiveness of sin" are declared to us, we receive exactly that: forgiveness, life, and salvation. God's Word does what he says it does. When God says "You are forgiven," forgiveness is bestowed regardless of whether we believe we deserve or have earned it.

In fact, even our believing the gospel is the work of God the Holy Spirit. Here is how Luther, explained it: "I believe that I cannot by my own reason or strength believe in Jesus Christ, my Lord, or come to him; but the Holy Spirit has called me by the gospel, enlightened me with his gifts, sanctified and kept me in the true faith." What does this have to do with worship? The answer is that we could not know anything about Jesus or believe he is our God and Savior unless God's Spirit reveals this to us through his Word.

Likewise, this means that everything in the Christian church, all of her worship and life, is organized by the Spirit for the purpose and goal of delivering forgiveness in Jesus' name. Through his Word and gifts, we receive the good news that Jesus took our sin, death, and God-forsakenness on himself. He did this out of great love for us. When this is declared to us in the "for-you-ness" of the gospel, we are comforted and enlivened, and our consciences are put at peace. It does not mean that we are suddenly free of sin, but it does means that the Holy Spirit will not allow sin to destroy us. This is why worship is a matter of death and new life. Where the gospel is not preached "for you" and the gifts not delivered, sin continues to rule over us and death's power over us persists uninterrupted. But where the gospel of Jesus Christ and his gifts are delivered "for you," we can enjoy the comfort and hope that the Spirit is at work in and among us. He works in us through his Word. He gifts us with a flood of forgiveness every day. He creates faith and hope in us to the end that sin and death will not overwhelm and crush us. In this way we are set free. We are freed to gladly hear and learn God's Word. We can enjoy the sermon. We can sing and pray with joy. Then, rather than worship being an experience that causes us to groan, it is the thing that undergirds our whole life.

This is what was missing, for me, during those early forays into churches. The primary message, and what I took away from worship at so many churches, was that my cooperation in my salvation made all the difference between whether I could hope for heaven or whether I needed to dread hell. My worship, my works, and my devotion were the primary ingredients. Jesus was mentioned, but as an example of faithful obedience to God's will. The Holy Spirit was mentioned too, as an impersonal force that empowers and enables me to cooperate with God in my salvation. The Father was mentioned on occasion, too, but as Almighty Judge or passive-aggressive father figure. The gospel and the gifts were talked about. People paid lip service to their importance, but they were notably absent when the conversation turned toward why we are Christians and why we gather for worship.

When we give up on ourselves, we get the direction of worship right. God has come down to us so we do not have to go up to him. He comes as giver and gift. He comes in the "for-you-ness" of his Son's life, death, and resurrection. He reveals himself to us in this way so we may be turned from sin and death to receive new life in Jesus' name. There is no need for us to transact a deal with God that will spare us his righteous judgment, as if this is even possible. Jesus has set us free from sin, death, and hell by exchanging his righteousness for ours. By his bloody suffering and death, Jesus sets us free from worry about whether God is for or against us. He sets us free from useless worship and sets us free from religion.

CHAPTER 6

FREEDOM: THE MOST VULGAR WORD IN THE BIBLE

When I thought of freedom, I thought of choice. The more choices that were available to me, the freer I was to enjoy all life had to offer. Take away my choices and you take away my freedom. That is how I ended up a slave. I was so free that I chose to give away my choices in order to consume alcohol. I was so free that I chose to give away my choices in order to consume opioids. I was so free that I let my addictions make choices for me, even though it meant my family could not trust me, friends kept me at arm's length, and I stole from everyone who believed my lies and employed me.

By the time I realized my error, it was too late. Addiction had consumed me. My refrigerator was empty. Drug dealers were after me. There was a bench warrant issued for my arrest. (I had failed to show up for a court date.) I had an expired license and no insurance. I had written so many bad checks no bank would allow me to open an account. That is when I accepted that I was powerless over alcohol and drugs and was out of options.

I was a twenty-three-year-old atheist, addict, and outlaw. I had spun a web of lies and half-truths. I deceived family, conned friends, and juggled multiple girlfriends in an attempt to feed the ever-increasing demands of my addiction. Whoever could give me money, alcohol, drugs, or a place to hide from responsibilities I treated as the most important person in the world. I professed my love for them. I said whatever I thought they wanted to hear, so long as I got what I needed. At some point, the choices, lies, and people could not distract me from the truth: I was not free. I was a slave. I was an addict.

I know that not all readers can relate to the dynamics of addiction, but what I have found is that we all are addicts of some sort. We are all hardwired to succumb to addiction, especially addiction to self. We are born lazy and greedy. We want the whole world, but we want everyone else to give it to us. When that does not happen, and we are mature enough to realize the world is not fair, that is when we use the ideas of freedom and choice as a cover for selfishness. Whatever, and whoever, we can use to justify what our selfish heart wants, we will use them, and we make up excuses for our failures. The excuse I used was that I was a victim. I did not slip through the cracks; I was born there. It was not my fault I drank so much; it was my dad's. He was an abusive alcoholic. Teachers were to blame for my bad grades. It was the police who were to blame for my mistrust of authority. It was my boss's fault I got fired. It was her fault that we broke up. She did not understand me or love me the way I needed to be loved. Sad me. Victim me. Selfish me.

This is the way I thought for a long time, even after conversion. But how about you? Can you relate? Maybe you think you can't. Maybe you grew up in a Christian home and were raised by loving parents. Regardless, you still have your problems. Maybe it's jealousy, narcissism, anger, and so on. Whatever our problems, the root of them is our view of God. We have got a problem with God being God for us. We would prefer to stand in God's place. We all have a God problem because we have not grasped what passivity and freedom mean. Let me explain.

Our God problem—our problem with the way Jesus does everything for our salvation as we do nothing—is that we think we somehow get to be active in our salvation. We refuse to die to self and passively accept Jesus' work on our behalf. We do not want to be passive in our salvation. We do not want Jesus to run all the verbs of salvation. We do not actually want to be set free from our slavish addiction to self-salvation.

Take, for example, Jesus' interaction with Nicodemus in John 3:1–21. When Jesus tells Nicodemus that only by being born again through water and the Spirit can he enter the kingdom of God, Nicodemus is stunned and confused. The reason for this is simple. Every morning, Nicodemus woke up and asked himself, "What must I do today to be saved? What must I do to be saved from my own selfish cravings and death and eternity separated from God? What must I do today to earn God's attention and favor?" Every day, the answer is the same: "I must do what God commands. I must be obedient to God's holy law." Nicodemus' whole life, day after day, month after month, year after tedious year, was decision after decision after decision. He hoped his decisions would add up to everything working out alright for him. Then Jesus came along and upended everything Nicodemus believes about God, the law, and his decisions. Jesus revealed that all Nicodemus' decisions had not brought him one inch closer to God's kingdom.

What baffled Nicodemus, the religious leaders, and religious people in general was that Jesus did not come to approve of Nicodemus's religiosity. Obedience training is not what Jesus had come to sell. A do-more-better attitude would not get anyone one inch closer to God's kingdom. Jesus did not come to improve upon Nicodemus' religion or to create a new religion. Jesus came to set Nicodemus free from religion.

This is why Nicodemus was so confused by Jesus. Nicodemus was a very religious man. His whole life was about believing, behaving, worshiping, and sacrificing to get right with God. But no amount of effort could take away his sin. No amount of effort could perfectly obey God's law. Everything Nicodemus did to try to do to get right with God was already being done by Jesus. And

everything Jesus has done is freely given to us by way of God's
Word combined with water and the Holy Spirit in baptism.

Baptism is God's sign that, as Robert Capon put it, the religion shop is out of business. And since God's not in the religion
business, his children are not either. We are baptized into the
gospel-preaching business. We are not baptized so we can bring
the world the bad news that God will think kindly about people
only after they have jumped through the right creedal, liturgical,
and moral hoops.

When Jesus speaks about baptism, he is talking about being
born again "from above" through the action of God (John 3:3).
St. Paul also expresses our passivity in relation to being born
again when he explains to the Roman Christians that we are buried with Jesus in baptism and raised with Jesus by God the Father
to live a new life (Romans 6:5). God saves us by making us passive recipients (when we are born, and born again, we are passive
objects) who receive Jesus' saving work for us. In the same way,
when God sends us a preacher, he sends him to pour the water "of
regeneration and renewal in the Holy Spirit" over us (Titus 3:5).
Our baptism into Christ means any and all requirements for being
a child of God are ended. Everything Jesus has done for us is given
to us in baptism for no religious purpose at all. It is all gift from
the Father for us. In baptism, Jesus' works are made our works.
His faithfulness is made our faith. His self-giving love is made our
love. His hope in the Father's mercy is made our hope.

Rather than work ourselves to death we get to enjoy God's baptismal freedom. We get to enjoy walking always in God's watery
forgiveness and love for us. We get to enjoy using baptism in
daily life, living in God's baptismal grace today and always. We are
baptized, and in spite of our best efforts to dress up God's baptismal grace in religious clothes, Jesus promises us that even when
we are faithless, he is faithful. That means no matter what crosses
are laid on us, no matter the struggles and afflictions we suffer,
no matter our lowest low or highest high, everything is going to
work out because we are baptized into Christ Jesus.

Now, as if passivity was not insult enough, we come to the most vulgar word in the Bible: freedom. In God's watery forgiveness, we are set free. But free to do what, we ask. Free to sin? Free from having to deal with the world and all its messes? Free from temptation and trials? No, we are set free by baptism to live for our neighbor. Now that we are washed into salvation, we do not have to worry about how we get to God. We do not have to worry about who God will be for us. We are off the hook for forgiveness, life, and eternal salvation. It is all gift. And now that we can stop chewing our nails about how God regards us, we can get on with the purpose and goal of life. Since we are perfectly passive in relation to our salvation, we are set free in baptism to use our freedom to love and encourage our neighbor.

Luther explains this well in his treatise, *The Freedom of a Christian*. "A Christian is a perfectly free lord of all, subject to none," he wrote. At the same time, he continued, "A Christian is a perfectly dutiful servant of all, subject to all." Here, Luther is working from Paul's assertion (Colossians 9:19), "for though I am free with respect to all, I have made myself a slave to all." The Christian life, as opposed to a religious life, is grounded in freedom. Paul says that we are free "with respect to *all*." He then says we are "a slave to *all*." This means we must not confuse God's baptismal promise and work with other salvation stories. Here the apostle drops absolutes, not conditions. He is not saying, "If you do well with your freedom, you will earn the reward of eternal life." He is not arguing, "If you do not nail this slave to all thing, God will punish you in this life and the next." Instead, Paul lays out that baptism creates a double sense of self. I am sinful in myself but righteous in Christ Jesus. I am Old Adam and New Man in Christ at the same time. I am totally freed from all worry about what I must do and leave undone to be saved. At the same time, I am totally bound to serve everyone as Jesus has loved and served me, in a selfless, self-giving way.

The Holy Spirit and baptism (and the faith he creates therein) obliterate all our religious hopes and dreams. Not even death can scare us now. We are free, even from the sting of death. We are also free from God's word of Law with all its increasing of trespasses. Now that we are free to cling to God's baptismal promises, the law's demands mean nothing to God. Now all that matters is his Word. We receive and trust his promises in Christ Jesus, because, "If the Son makes you free, you will be free indeed" (John 8:36).

"You will be free." This is God's promise to us. The Son comes to us, ungodly, enemies of God, chained up by Satan in the dungeon of sin and death. He breaks into the strongman's house to set us free from sin, death, and hell. It is a watery rescue. But in the "washing of regeneration and renewal of the Holy Spirit" (Titus 3:5), we lose any and all slavery to the Law's demands. We become like an addict, in a sense. When Jesus translates us into his kingdom, we lose our strength and will to be our own savior. Instead, we are possessed by God's Spirit in a way that creates faith in us to trust that Jesus' strength and will sets him over us as our Savior.

Since God has come to us, we do not have to find him. This may seem like a no-brainer, but once we hear he chooses to be for us, it is not so easy to say our amen. We do not seek God, and we do not need to locate him. He locates himself for us in simple, earthly words, water, bread, and wine. He makes himself available to us as Giver and Gift, including his Word, his Spirit, and his body and blood for us. We do not have to leave our relation to God up to chance, luck, fate, or hard work. He chooses to announce himself to us when and where he chooses, in a concrete, real way. The preacher God sends, and the means his Spirit chooses to call, gather, and enlighten us are how he will be known by us.

We are thereby set free by God's watery promise to praise him and mock the devil. We are so free we even get to thumb our nose at death. And what is more offensive to people hard at work on escaping judgment and eternal death than a free person joking about sin and death? That is why freedom is so vulgar to those who struggle every day to work out their salvation with fear and trembling, apart from faith in Christ Jesus. Jesus announces to us, through his preachers, grace that forgives all sin, a baptismal new life raised from death, and eternal life. We do not need more time and choices, it turns out, to be free. We need more Jesus.

God, in his kindness, was patient with me. It took me a long time to acknowledge that the point of Christianity is not to get busy doing religious things, but to receive as gift all that Jesus has done for me. As I noted in earlier chapters, before I had even made up my mind whether there was a God or not, I did whatever I could to learn about God. I wanted to figure out for myself whether God was real, whether he was involved personally in my life, and what I needed to do to get him off my back. Several years later, after I had become a Christian of a sort, that passion shifted to overt religious actions. As a missionary, I worked sixty to eighty hours a week. I taught music and choir. I volunteered at the mission's free clinic. I went on daily outreach trips into migrant camps. I played in three praise bands at the local church. I was a reserve firefighter, and on and on. If there was something I could do to prove myself to God and my peers, I jumped at the opportunity.

When my time at the mission was up and I ended up in Portland, Oregon, my zeal was undiminished. In fact, my opinion was that amongst Christian friends I was the only true believer, because I was the only one who seemed the least bit concerned about living a righteous, god-pleasing life. Unlike people at church, I felt compelled to "do" all things religious—to serve, worship, preach, and teach. I did my best to "walk the walk" of a true Christian. But my zeal blinded me to the truth. I was running away from Jesus in order to worship God.

My sin is most clearly illustrated by Jesus' encounter with the ten lepers recounted in Luke 17:11–19. The lepers see Jesus, and from a distance they shout at him, begging him to help them. Jesus comes near and says to them that they must go and present themselves to the local priests. The ten lepers obey Jesus' command. As they go to the temple, they are cleansed. Nine go to see the priests. They follow Jesus' commands to the letter. Their obedience is remarkable. But one turns back. He is a Samaritan, making him a foreigner and outsider. He ignores Jesus' command. Instead, he looks for Jesus. When he finds him, he falls on his knees and worships Jesus. It is the who turns back, the Samaritan, Jesus says, who is saved. So, what are we supposed to learn from this man? We learn from Jesus' encounter with the lepers that God does not want us to focus attention on our obedience, but to focus on Jesus' freely given grace instead.

The Samaritan is thankful. He comes back to worship Jesus. The other nine do not recognize that Jesus is God. So they go to the temple instead. Their faith points them in the wrong direction, and they end up running away from God. They begin with Jesus, but end up turning their back on him by trying to complete the work he began.

The Samaritan's faith points him in the right direction, to Jesus. He runs back to God because he recognizes that God has already come to find him. He begins with Jesus and ends with Jesus. He is not going to try to complete what Jesus starts. He recognizes that "God is reconciling the world to himself in his Son, Jesus Christ." That is why the Samaritan's faith saved him.

What Jesus teaches when he cleanses the lepers makes for a "your faith has saved you" lesson. The Samaritan is not just healed by Jesus. He is cleansed and forgiven, and so he is saved. Jesus saves him. The Samaritan's Jesus saves him, and that is the way it is with God. If our faith is pointed in the right direction, we can swap back and forth between "faith" and "Jesus." Jesus says to the one, "Stand up and go your way. Your faith has saved you." That is the same as if Jesus were to say, "Stand up and go your way. Your Jesus has saved you."

Jesus' cleansing of the lepers is more of a "your Jesus has saved you" lesson or, better yet, a "Jesus for you" lesson. However, this is not just a lesson about what Jesus does for these men along the border between Samaria and Galilee. This is about what Jesus is doing for us in the present along the border between sin and death and forgiveness and life. It is the same today. Jesus comes to us here and now. He comes to cleanse us of all sin. He comes to send us on our way cleansed and forgiven so we can love each other with the same self-giving, self-sacrificing love Jesus shows us. He comes to fill our ears and throat, fill the whole of us, with his promise and gifts. He comes to say, "God doesn't remember your sin anymore." He comes to give us salvation.

Jesus' whole engagement with the lepers is about the "for-you-ness" of Jesus—God here, now, for us. Words. Water. Bread. Wine. It is all for us so he can say to us, too, "Go your way. Your Jesus saves you." We are set free to go our way. We are graced by God baptismally, given a new life in Christ Jesus. Eternal salvation is our certain hope. All from God the great giver to us as gift. He even gives us his faith—he gives us our Jesus—so we may believe the truth about his work for us and what follows from it.

It all begins at baptism. In baptism, we have already been put to death with Christ Jesus. In baptism, we have been raised to walk in a new life. This new life means we see ourselves as two people at the same time. As I noted in the previous chapter, we are set free in baptism so that we are no longer slaves to sin, death, and Satan. In Christ, through faith, we are masters of all. In baptism, we are declared "saints," raised from death, free from all sin and judgment to live under Jesus in his kingdom in righteousness, innocence, and blessedness now and always. At the same time, we are sinful, dead, and powerless to do anything about the power of sin at work in us or the judgment that God promises will come.

We are, however, set free from these worries. "Baptism now saves you," writes Peter (1 Peter 3:21). For the new man in Christ, past and future do not exist. They are illusions, lies, false realities that occupy old Adam's attention, but for the new man in Christ, there is only the now of baptismal "regeneration and renewal in the Holy Spirit" (Titus 3). For the new man in Christ, baptism now saves you. This is not a past event with future consequences.

Baptism is a past event, with present tense consequences, that continue into the future and eternity.

Baptism then informs a Christian's daily life. All the vocations that God calls him to are founded on and informed by God's baptismal promise. This new life that is so alien to the old Adam and the world sets a Christian free to serve his neighbor without worry about whether God will smile upon his work. He exists now to serve his neighbor in selfless, self-giving love.

This new reality means fear is off the table, as is insecurity about the past, present, and future. What is there to worry about when we have already been judged in baptism, and the judgment was "you are reconciled to God for Christ's sake . . . Baptism now saves you"? God does not need our good works, but our neighbor does. A Christian has been put to death in baptism, and a new man is raised to live before our heavenly Father as his beloved child.

Since we are reconciled with God through his baptismal work for us we have a lot of time on our hands waiting for Jesus' return. So, in the meantime, God goes to work in and through us to produce the fruits of salvation, not for our sake but our neighbor's. We are baptized into Christ, and therefore we are made right with God. We are a "good tree" now because the Spirit's work produces good fruit. This is not intended for us to turn the Spirit's work into a new list of good works for us to earn our way back into God's good graces. Instead, we receive this good news about trees and fruit as God's baptismal promise to us.

We are freed from saving ourselves, earning eternal rewards, and escaping judgment and death so that we may focus on everyone except ourselves. We do not have to chase after God anymore. We do not have to worry over good works. We are freed from worrying about ourselves. We are free as much as Jesus is free since he lives in us now. This life, just as Jesus demonstrated with his own life, is lived outside ourselves in Christ Jesus.

Instead of worrying all the time about whether we are worthy of God's grace and attention God reveals to us that he is intimately involved in his world, locating himself right in the middle of everyday life. God is at work in marriages, in procreation and birth, in every home and community, in planting and harvest, work and rest, arts and culture. We do not have to go looking for a higher, spiritual calling to enjoy a right relationship with God. When we receive our vocations in faith, our whole lives are worship.

Think about God's work in a home. First, God gives a man and woman to each other in marriage. Then he gives them a child or five. The parents need to love their children. Their children need to be fed and clothed. They need a safe, warm place to sleep. They need to be protected from themselves, the world, and the forces of hell. How does this good life take shape? God does it all for them. Marriage, home, food, clothing, love, and safety are the ways God works in our home to care and provide for his creation.

But what about sin? As much as we may love our family members, and enjoy the vocations God has placed us in, we are sinfully selfish. Our selfish, self-serving need to worry about ourselves always gets in the way of serving our neighbor in love. That is why it is so important to see our self as simultaneously sinful and righteous. Sinners are selfish. It is our default position. It is everyone's default position. But only the Christian is simultaneously sinful in the flesh and righteous in Christ through faith. Since we live in this tension, we admit that God needs to step in to protect us from ourselves, our neighbors from us, and us from our neighbors.

In the world, God's word of law orders and restrains us. We must serve our neighbor for his good, and the law will make sure this happens. God's word of law defines life and what we owe to God by way of fear, love, and trust. We must love God and love our neighbor—the two tables of the Ten Commandments. God's word of law tells us what we owe God and neighbor, but it does not give us the ability to do it. The law cannot give to us what it demands.

Now that we are put right with God through baptism and faith we see ourselves and the world in a new way. We do not love

God and neighbor because we must. We love God and neighbor because we are called to them through the gospel. It is Christ in us, as Paul writes in Galatians 2:20, that calms our worry about whether we are doing right by God and our neighbor. Freed from worry about judgment, not measuring up, and failure we are led by Christ Jesus into our vocations. It is here that God works through us for the benefit of others. He will provide for them by working through us. Simultaneously, God uses the needs of our neighbor to pull us out of our selfish, self-seeking ways. We are created to love God and each other, not to use God and our neighbor to love ourselves. We are made to stand face-to-face, look each other in the eye, and say, "Brother, what do you need from me?" Seeing things and serving in this way is only possible in view of the freedom won for us by Jesus when he declared, on the cross, that God's good and great work for us was finished (John 19:30). At that moment, the religion(s) men and women have invented over the ages were crucified and our emancipation from fear of sin, death, and the devil was brought to completion by God in the person and work of his son, Jesus Christ.

CHAPTER 7

JESUS: THE KEY TO UNDERSTANDING THE BIBLE

There is one more thing I feel I must add for those who have made it this far in the book. I am convinced that the theology I received from Augustine, Luther, C.S. Lewis, Pastor Kreuger, and others—the theology I've described up until now—is entirely grounded in the scriptures. However, as you no doubt know, the Bible is interpreted in so many different ways. So before wrapping this up I offer here my suggestions for those who are like I was, trying to sort out what to believe about God.

As I noted in the first chapter, when I first read the Bible it was difficult to understand. Actually, it was incomprehensible. I did not know where to start. I could not seem to get a foothold anywhere. From Genesis to Matthew's gospel, to Philemon and 1 John, I was looking for something, anything, that could show me which way to God.

My experience was not uncommon. Many people I have talked to over the years have voiced a similar struggle. They ask, "When I read the Bible, what am I looking for? What is the point?" "I was taught in Sunday school that BIBLE stands for Basic Instructions Before Leaving Earth. Is that true?" "Is the Bible a series of illustrations of holy men and women, whose example I'm supposed to follow if I want to get into God's good graces?" "Can the Bible help as a guide for those who are doing their best to live a good life?" "If I try to live my life the way the Bible teaches, is there any hope for me that God will fill in the spots with his grace and mercy where I make a mess of things?" These are the questions that I have been and continue to be asked but those still seeking to understand God and his disposition towards his creation.

When I first read the Bible, and for many years thereafter, I did not so much seek to understand God's Word as I wanted to overstand God's Word. What I mean by this is that I went into the Bible to find solutions to my problems with God, my friends, family, and myself. I went through the Bible hoping to collect data that could help me out of the troubles my addiction had created for me. I wanted the Bible to lay out for me what was the point of life, the universe, and everything. Which God was the real God? What happens after we die? How do I change my doomed existence into something worthy of God's love and attention?

When we read the Bible seeking answers to these questions we actually end up attacking God's Word. We fail to realize the true intent of God's Word for us because, although we can judge the basic meaning of the biblical texts easy enough, we fail to understand the purpose and goal of God's Word. More than that, though, despite our best efforts at interpretation, in the end only God's Spirit can reveal the truth of scripture to us. We must pray that God lifts the sinful veil from our eyes. What we will find is that the Bible is less about us and more about Jesus. In fact, what we find is that Jesus is the primary purpose and goal of all scripture. This makes all the difference for us when we go into the Bible.

A perfect and common example of how we often go searching for personal meaning in the Bible centers on the topic of predestination and election. When Christians read the Bible and encounter a text that speaks specifically about predestination, as in Romans 8:29, they get hung up on the question about whether God numbers them among the elect. The next question usually involves what they must do to prove to themselves and other Christians that they are, in fact, predestined for heaven rather than hell. This is a topic that strikes at the very heart of old Adam sinners. It is troubling because at its core the question exposes to us that we are not in control of our destiny as much as we may convince ourselves otherwise.

An example from the life of Luther will help illustrate this. In his *Letters of Spiritual Council*, Luther responds to a laywoman, Barbara Lisskirchen, who is troubled about what she has been taught about predestination.[4] He counsels her to consider what God's Word says about election. In particular, he encourages her to consider predestination evangelically in relation to Christ and his cross.

First, Luther points out that her struggle is an invitation to unbelief from the devil himself. It is a "fiery dart" from the evil one (Ephesians 6:16) that Luther had himself experienced. The whole matter of predestination, in the hands of old Adam sinners, is a temptation to investigate matters that God does not preach and reveal to us. Luther uses Psalm 131:1 ("my eyes are not raised too high; I do not occupy myself with things too great for me") to direct Barbara away from what God has concealed from human understanding. In short, Luther warns, we are not to pry into those areas where God does not want to be preached, revealed, and worshiped in Christ Jesus. Second, he urges Barbara to learn to ask herself, "In which commandment is it written that I should think about and deal with this matter?" He directs her to use the first commandment against Satan, because at the root of her anxiety about predestination and election is a devilish attack. This is not small thing, Luther warns, because the truth is she is engaged in spiritual warfare. Third, if the question about

---

[4] Martin Luther, *Luther: Letters of Spiritual Counsel*, translated by Theodore G. Tappert (Vancouver: Regent College Publishing, 2003).

predestination and election continues to torment her, she is to be persistent and refuse to give up. "In this way you must always put these thoughts away from you and turn your attention to God's Commandments." Fourth, she is to focus on Christ crucified. "The highest of all God's commands is this, that we hold before our eyes the image of his dear Son, our Lord Jesus Christ." At this final point Luther concludes with a benediction: "May our dear Lord Jesus Christ show you his hands and his side and gladden your heart with his love, and may you behold and hear him until you find your joy in him."

What Luther essentially does in this letter is to urge Barbara to approach the teaching of election in and through Christ Jesus. In this way, we do not use the Bible to prove that the doctrine of election is a teaching that comes before Christ crucified. Instead, we understand the question as an aftereffect of the fact that Jesus alone is the God and Lord who saves sinners. Using the New Testament's imagery of Christ alone as the foundation, Luther remarks that Christians start with the foundation (Christ) and not the roof (predestination):

> In Christ, God has furnished us with a foundation, on which to stand and from which we can go up to heaven. He is the only way and the only gate which leads to the Father. If we despise this foundation and in the devil's name start building at the roof, we shall surely fall.

Learning from Luther, it is important that we understand God's Spirit is the active player in the matter of predestination and election. God acts through the scriptures. The scriptures are the Word of God. They are not just words about God but the Word from God. This means that we must distinguish, when we read God's Word, between human words about God and words spoken from God. Human words search for meaning, but God's Word does what he says it does. This distinction is impossible for us. In our religious zeal to locate meaning for our lives, we actually end up using the Bible as a defense mechanism against

JESUS: THE KEY TO UNDERSTANDING   95

God. When old Adam sinners get religion, like I did, we use the scriptures as a tool by which we bring God to heel. Our interpretations, which are just theories in search of solid footing, are used to make God our debtor. But then we are caught in a trap of our own design. We construct a theory about God's relation to us that is supposed to win God over by its attractiveness. But that is not the purpose and goal of God's Word. The intent of God's Word is to foster the preaching of God's promise of Christ crucified for the sin of the world.

Christ Jesus embodies all of Holy Scripture. He pries open the seals that were shut and reveals the will of God. Scripture is not interested in presenting us with theories for how to live a pious Christian life in relation to our God. God is concerned with the proclamation of the death and resurrection of Jesus for the forgiveness of sin. Because of Christ and the giving of the Holy Spirit all of the scriptures have been unlocked and therefore are clear for the proclamation of the forgiveness of sin. God's Word is clear about this. We are the ones who are deluded and confused.

God's saving of us old Adam sinners is the purpose and goal of holy scripture. God's Word comes to godless people so we may receive Jesus Christ for the forgiveness of sin and eternal salvation. Yes, there is much hidden from us by God, but there is nothing hidden in God's revelation of the Son. Because of Christ, all scripture is revealed to us and is clear for the proclamation of the gospel. In Jesus, everything we need to know about God is preached and revealed to us because in Christ is the "fullness of the image of God" (Colossians 1:15). Likewise, as Jesus says, "You search the scriptures because you think that in them you have eternal life; and it is they that bear witness about me" (John 5:39). And most important for our understanding of the whole Bible, Jesus is the Word of God who makes God known to us because, as John writes, "No one has ever seen God, but the one and only Son, who is himself God and is at the Father's side, has made him known" (John 6:46).

John's gospel especially reveals that Jesus makes God known to us, and Jesus in turn is running loose in the whole of scripture. What you read in the Old Testament, all the works and promises of God, all the ways through which he chooses to give himself to his people for their salvation, they all come true in God's Christ, the Word born of the virgin, Jesus. The Word of God, the second person of the Trinity, Jesus is at work throughout history and in the present in the word of the gospel, waters of baptism, and his flesh and blood under the bread and wine.

God is present at all times in all places because God's Word creates time and space. That means when God's preacher announces the gospel of Jesus Christ to us in the present tense, God's Word is simultaneously speaking to Abraham in the past and, at the same time, raising us up into the resurrection at the last day in Christ Jesus. For this reason, when Christians sing with the heavenly choir of angels, and all the company of heaven, "Holy, Holy, Holy" (Isaiah 6:3) in the historical liturgy of the church, we are all singing with our great-great-grandparents who we have never met, with grandchildren we will never meet, and with all the saints in the resurrection because in Christ all time is now. On account of God's Word being present tense for us at all times and places, we locate ourselves in two times: linear time, which is marked by our birth and death, and non-linear time, which is marked by the now-ness of God's Word.

All God gives us is today. God gives us to the day, and all he gives to us is for today. Just like God provided manna for the Israelites in the wilderness day by day, we receive the Lord's Supper each week. This is where God's Word is for us in the present tense. He provides us with all the earthly gifts we need for our body and life. He also gives himself to us for our salvation. God's Word is giver and gift through the words that come out of his preacher's mouth, through the waters of baptism, and through the bread and wine at the Lord's Supper. Therefore, what Seth, Noah, Abraham, Moses, and Isaiah preached is the same Word of God, inspired by the same Spirit, that Augustine, Luther, and every preacher speaks as he is moved by God's Spirit.

If we try to locate ourselves as the subject of the Bible, or at least read the Bible as a set of instructions that set us up to act as our own savior, we end up pushing the Son in particular out of the biblical witness. Then God's Word is pushed outside of the Bible, outside time and space, so that he is not present in history for us. If Jesus is not active and real in history, then God's Word is not active and real for us in the present tense. If God's Word is not concrete and real for us, then do we really want to go to church? What is the point if God is not going to speak to us? Do we even bother to leave the house? It is a violent and chaotic world where God is not present for us. And what about our vocations? What is the meaning of our work? Do they only serve to keep us from doing great violence to each other? Do they exist to keep us civilized? Without God's active, real, and concrete Word what is our value to others and ourselves? Is our belief in God and love for each other summed up by, "You get out of it what you put into it"?

Every religion I have studied essentially teaches that there is a god, goddess, or gods that have made us and put us here to serve them and to be subject to their whims. The entire purpose of our lives is to be tested by the gods. Depending on how we do on the test, we are either elevated to paradise or thrown down into hell. But we never know how close we are to either because life is a test, and the final grade is hidden from us until the judgment day. Christianity is different. The Christian life is what we might call a sacramental faith. Living out of a sacramental faith means we are created and put here so that God can love us and serve us. The direction of our religion and worship is not from us to God. It is not a sacrificial religion at all but a sacramental faith. That means we trust in God's giving to us and his sacrifices for us. God's Word dwells among us, as John 1:14 teaches, and as long as God's Word is living, active, and busy in his creation, speaking all things into being, we do not define life in terms of a religious, sacrificial life.

Life is not a test. Instead, life is a gift that the love of God reveals to us through Jesus crucified for our sin. He wants to be known by us as a loving Father and to know ourselves as his beloved children. In this way, all of life is revealed to us to be a gift. Even crosses and afflictions can be received as gift now because we have been chosen to suffer as our Lord suffered. We can say with the apostle, "To live is Christ and to die is gain" (Philippians 1:21). We suffer and are afflicted as Jesus suffered and was afflicted, and we gain Jesus, because the crosses and afflictions are lifted off us in death.

This means that the nature of our vocation changes too. We do not serve our neighbor because God is watching us, keeping score of our good and bad works. We serve our neighbor because we recognize God in our neighbor through faith in Christ Jesus. This all hinges, of course, on whether we follow the biblical witness and locate God's Word, the man Jesus, in time and active in creation for us. If we do this, then even on our worst day we remain gifts from God for our neighbor because "I have been crucified with Christ. It is no longer I who live, but Christ who lives in me. And the life I now live in the flesh I live by faith in the Son of God, who loved me and gave himself for me" (Galatians 2:20).

But when we operate out of scarcity, out of our fear and insecurities about our eternal destiny, then we read the Bible sacrificially. We read it asking, "What must I do to inherit eternal life?" We look for where God says, "Do that. That was some good stuff, but don't do that other stuff. That's no good." But when we operate out of abundance, out of the comfort and assurance that comes to us from God's Word, who promises forgiveness, life, and salvation to his beloved people, then we can receive each other as gifts because we are all one in Christ Jesus.

CHAPTER 8

WHEN GOD'S LAW AND THE GOSPEL GET AHOLD OF US

It was several years after my conversion that I heard the present tense, for-youness of the gospel preached. It was my old pastor and mentor, Stephen Kreuger, who God first used to give me the good news about Jesus. Before him, I had heard hundreds of sermons. But they had all been sermons that delivered a doable version of the Ten Commandments. And when Jesus was mentioned he was depicted as a teacher of a Christian form of the law, as illustrated many times by pastors who preached on the Beatitudes or, as some like to call them, the "Be-Attitudes." After years of listening to such sermons, it was a shock to hear a pastor proclaim that on account of Jesus all my sin is forgiven. Even more stunning, in his sermons he punctuated every announcement of Jesus' saving work with a "for you." He would say, "Jesus did this for you," "Jesus died for you," and so on.

Sitting in that uncomfortable wooden pew every Sunday, six rows back from the pulpit, I would lean forward and grip the back of the pew in front of me excited for what I knew was going to happen. I was like a sheep eager for his shepherd to call to him. I wanted that Gospel for-youness. I hungered for the words that

declared all my sin forgiven with no added conditions or stipula-
tions. On those cold, damp Oregon mornings I could not wait for
him to get into the pulpit and preach a word that revealed and
condemned my sin and then drowned that same damnable sin in
Jesus' precious blood and innocent suffering and death.

Thanks to Pastor Krueger and several theologians since, who
taught me how to listen for God's Word of law and gospel, and
how to read the Scripture in this way, too, I do not go into the
Bible, church, or the pulpit seeking ways to save myself. Instead,
I pray God will give me the strength to distinguish his word of
law and gospel, that I can hear his word of law lawfully and his
Gospel evangelically and that he would allow the proper distinction of his word of law and gospel to color my reading of the
Bible. Otherwise, it is not difficult to imagine how easily I can
be overrun by my selfish need to save myself and use the pious
cover of Jesus' name to do it.

It is not difficult for me to imagine because it has happened—to
myself and others. I have interacted with many people over the
years and built an entire theology on the false assumption that
God commands us to cherish and obey his commandments. And
since God commands it, we must have the ability to cherish and
obey his holy law. But is that the point of God's commandments?
No. All of God's commandments and commands, show us what
the power of sin has done to us and how sin controls our every
decision and action. We are "under the power of sin," as St. Paul
writes (Romans 3:9). This is our condition. We are sold under
sin. Sin rules us. We serve sin. We have no choice. Sin is going to
kill us, and there is nothing we can do to stop it. This is why the
apostle cries out, "Wretched man that I am! Who will deliver me
from the body of this death?" (Romans 7:24).

Contrary to our false assumptions about our abilities, God
actually does command the impossible to stop us dead in our
tracks. When God's Word speaks a command, he shows us
our inability to believe and obey as he commands us to believe
and obey with perfect obedience and trust from our hearts.

When God commands us, for example, to repent and believe the gospel, he does not want us to respond with, "Okay, I'll get right on that. And, don't worry, I'm going to do my best. You'll see." What God's Word wants is for us to say, "But . . . that's impossible!" Only then—when God's Word reveals to us that we have nothing to offer him—are we ready to receive God's Word as our Christ.

This scriptural understanding of God's commandments is vital for Christian faith. We are under the power of sin. We have been sold into slavery to sin. We have lost our ability to choose between God and the devil, faith and unbelief, grace and sin, promise and Law, blessing and curse. We are compelled by the power of sin to always disobey and disbelieve God is God for us. And worse, when we assume we are free to choose between good and bad, right and wrong, belief and obedience to God's commandments, we are actually standing in the place of God, knowing good and evil. We are not being obedient to God's commands. Instead, we are reenacting the original sin. Only when God exposes our sin and we are tempted to give up hope of ever being saved from our doo, can we receive his faithful, loving kindness that comes to us in the person of the Son, Jesus the Christ.

God's commands are good because they are his. But as St. Paul writes, "sin, seizing an opportunity through the commandment, deceived me and through it killed me" (Romans 7:11). It is not the commandments but sin that deceives us, inspiring us to imagine we can do and not do what God commands. Sin stirs us up to believe we can be good and holy, just as God is good and holy. We imagine we can be like God, if we can only be more faithful and obedient. Sin sells us on the lie that we have the ability and freedom to choose to obey God's commands.

When this happens, we even imagine that God's faithful, loving-kindness is extended to us for the purpose of encouraging faithful obedience. We imagine God's graciousness is a spiritual steroid injected into us by his Spirit to strengthen us for a life of perfect obedience. All this does, though, is drive us away

(Romans 3:31).

God's Word demands we be do-ers of his commandments, not try-ers. He does not wink at our sin either. His commands put us in an impossible position, which is exactly where he wants us. He wants to expose the power of sin in our lives and our lawless ungodliness. Why? Because God's Word loves to justify the ungodly (Romans 4:5)! It is not what God commands but what the Son has done to fulfill God's commands in our place that finally matters. We are not expected to be doers of God's command but believers in God's promise. His commands turn us away from ourselves and all our self-salvation projects to hear what he promises us through the Son: forgiveness for our lawlessness, life rising up out of sin-induced death, and salvation for those who have been shown they never had a chance at saving themselves by obeying God's commands.

When old Adam sinners organize their commentary on the Old Testament, the table of contents goes as follows:

- Chapter 1: Adam and Eve—How Not to Fail God's Test
- Chapter 2: How to Be Obedient Like Noah.
- Chapter 3: How to Be Faithful Like Abraham
- Chapter 4: Moses, Part 1—How to Be a Leader Like Moses
- Chapter 5: Moses, Part 2—How to Live in Obedience to God's Commands
- Chapter 6: The Prophets—How to Preach Judgment to Godless People
- Chapter 7: The Psalms—How to Repent and Pray Like David
- Chapter 8: How to Suffer for Righteousness's Sake Like Job, and the Rewards You Will Receive

- Chapter 9: How to Be Submissive Like Ruth (A Model for Christian Women)
- Chapter 10: How to Be Obedient Like Young David—Overcoming Our Personal Goliaths
- Chapter 11: How to Be Faithful Like King David—the Apple of God's Eye
- Chapter 12: How to Follow the Old Testament Saints' Example—a Summary of How to Pass the Test

It is easy to laugh at the absurdity of reading the Bible in this way, but the truth is that we old Adam sinners cannot help ourselves. We must make the Bible about us. We are compelled to push God's Word out of the spotlight. We, not the Son, must take center stage. We resist reading the Bible as being primarily about God's salvation of those who call him "enemy."

We do not want God to run the verbs of salvation. We old Adam sinners insist on running the verbs. We tell Jesus he is not in the game. Instead, he needs to go and sit at the end of the bench. When we run the verbs of salvation, the Bible becomes a disjointed group of stories written by men and women who have got a lot to lose if it does not conclude with a happy ending. We old Adam sinners use God's Word to try to turn our tragic biography of sin and death into a heroic narrative.

This is also why we old Adam sinners find an unacceptable Savior in Jesus. Jesus does not seem brave like Joshua. He is not dangerous like Gideon. He is not strong enough to take on our enemies. Where is a savior like Ehud when we need one? What good is Jesus? He suffers horrible pain and death. He comes not to be served, but to serve. We do not need a servant. We need a conquering hero. We need a godly example to follow. We look for the greatest moral example and hero.

We do this because we are trying to find a better version of ourselves in the Bible—the New Me 2.0. This is the "me" that does not need to suffer and die; the "me" we can look at in the mirror without fear, guilt, and revulsion; and the "me" we wish

Jesus would be for us—good me, brave me, undying me, God-me. What we find in the Old Testament, however, is remarkably immoral people loved by a promise-keeping, gift-giving God. Far from being about saintly morality and heroic faith, the Old Testament is one long history of God's faithful, loving kindness toward unlovable sinners.

The Bible does not invite us to search for examples of self-salvation. Every word of the Bible reveals God's Word, who pursues the godless. Every word of scripture testifies to God's Word and his work for sinners. God's Word runs all the verbs of salvation. God's Word creates faith and life where there is none. As Jesus says, "You search the scriptures because you think that in them you have eternal life; and it is they that bear witness about me" (John 5:39). Every page of the Old Testament proclaims, "Christ! Christ!" Therefore, the purpose of reading about the experiences of Abraham, Moses, David, the disciples, and so on is to learn about God's Word, who pursues even the worst sinners until they are brought to rest in God's love in Jesus. Every word of scripture preaches the faithfulness and love of Israel's Messiah for his chosen people.

This is a liberating change of direction for us self-absorbed sinners. When we are set free to read scripture as the history of God's Word active in his creation for his people, the weight we carry in regard to our eternal destiny simply falls off our shoulders. Abraham was godless when God came to him. Terah, Abraham, and their whole family lived right down the road from Babel. They worshiped the goddess Nana. God's Word came to Abraham and told him to leave his father and family. From Haran, Abraham inched his way down to Canaan alongside his family, friends, slaves, herds and livestock. He pitched his tent at Bethel, but a famine came. There was nothing to eat. No crops would grow. All the livestock dropped dead from disease and dehydration. Worse yet, Abraham was a stranger in a strange land. He did not speak the language so well. These alien peoples' customs were lost on him. He did not worship their gods. How would he survive?

God led Abraham down into Egypt. But Egypt was not as advertised on television. Egypt's eastern border was choked with refugees fleeing the famine. So, as a way to get past the border guards, Abraham tried to pass off his wife, Sarah, as his sister. What man of faith pimps out his wife and profits greatly from it? Maybe, to give Abraham the benefit of the doubt, it was a political gesture. Maybe it was not. Maybe Abraham just wanted to survive. Since he had left Ur, it had been one conflict after another. Afflictions and trials piled up on top of old afflictions and trials. How many times did Abraham have to hit rock bottom before God would say, "Okay, enough. You've sacrificed enough . . . and you just can't seem to nail down the whole obedience thing. Let's call it off. Thanks, though. I appreciate the effort!"

Even Sarah doubted God's integrity and indicted Abraham. "Abraham, this is all your fault! I put my servant, Hagar, in bed with you so we could help God's work along and welcome a son into our home. But instead, Hagar threw this in my face and hated me! I don't care what you do but fix it!" For twenty-five years Abraham and Sarah waited for God to speak to them. One horrible event after another weighed on Abraham. Where was the God who called Abraham out of his father's house? Where was the promise-making God? Where was their protector? Why did God not send them a preacher?

Then, one day, three men appeared to Abraham. God's Word renewed his promise and told Abraham, "You will have your son within a year." Abraham laughed so hard at this that he fell on his face. Sarah also laughed at the absurd promise she had just heard. How could a one hundred–year-old woman give birth to a son? Then Abraham went back again into enemy territory to survive. He went back to Negev, where they were confronted. Abraham fell back on an old tactic. He sold Sarah to Abimelech. She was only his sister, after all. God bailed Abraham out again. And so it went between Abraham and this strange God who pursued the wandering Aramean even when he was at his worst. He is the God Abraham eventually called, "Jehovah-Jireh," which means "God will provide."

When God came to Abraham, the man worshiped other gods. After God called Abraham, he stuttered and stumbled between trust and self-destructive, promise-shattering disbelief. And yet, God's Word covered all of Abraham's sin with the promise: "In your seed all the nations of the earth will be blessed, because you have listened to My voice." Abraham stuttered and stumbled through life, like any of us do. But, "For the promise to Abraham and his offspring that he would be heir of the world did not come through the law but through the righteousness of faith" (Romans 4:13).

We can worry endlessly about our piety, spirituality, moral progress, or what we must do to inherit eternal life. But all this does is cause us to fall victim to the temptation to make the Bible primarily about us. We can pray that the Father will over-shadow us with his Spirit so we are always turned toward the Son who makes God known to us. We can pray that the Son will interpret and translate us into his kingdom through his Spirit and promise. When he does this for us, then we are caught up into the narrative of God's faithful, loving kindness to his promises. When God's Word acts for us, then we are yoked together with him. He binds us to himself. Whether in Genesis or Romans, Leviticus or Galatians, we are held blessedly and joyfully captive by God's Word so we may perceive that every word of scripture is recorded to reveal Jesus to us as God and Savior. Then when we follow the lives of the Patriarchs or dig into a Parable, we are always asking, "Where's the Son? Where's the Christ? How do God's Word of law and gospel reveal Jesus dead and risen for me? How does this text deliver Christ Jesus for the forgiveness of sin for my comfort and consolation?" Then it is not us who have gotten ahold of God, as if we ever could do that, but it is God's Word who has gotten ahold of us in the best way of all—by the forgiveness of sin, life, and eternal salvation in his name.

If I dig down to the root of my search for meaning, my questions about the purpose and goal of life, and all my study of philosophy and religions, what I was hunting for the whole time was quiet and peace—the kind of quiet and peace that has only ever come to me through the forgiveness of sin in Jesus' name. That was God's answer two decades ago as I sat in a Roman Catholic cathedral on Good Friday and prayed, "God, don't make yourself known to me and then just let me sit here and be a pew warmer." His answer will always be my comfort and consolation, whether I am at rest or struggling, at peace or afflicted, faithful or faithless. His answer to me was simple: Jesus. Jesus is your comfort, consolation, and even when you are unfaithful he is faithful because he cannot deny himself (2 Timothy 2:13).

AFTERWORD

As I noted at the beginning, I wrote this book as much for myself as you, dear reader. For many years I prayed and hoped someone would help me find my way into the deep waters of the Christian faith. I did not so much want someone to provide me with all the right answers (although that was on my mind at the time), but I was in earnest about someone pointing me in the right direction for my questions. Too often in conversation with Christians I would be told, "This is the right theology" or "If you want to be a Christian, this is what you must believe." On some occasions I was told, "You really need to read this theologian" or "This book is amazing. It will change your life!" Some did; many did not. But I appreciated those who listened to my questions, gave honest answers, and pointed me toward the theologians, pastors, and thinkers who helped them with their faith questions. What I did not know at the time, but what became clear along the way, was that my questions begged for the gospel. I hungered and thirsted for righteousness.

The righteousness I initially craved was not the kind of righteousness I could find in the pages of a philosophical treatise, legal brief, or personal improvement project. I craved Jesus, the righteousness of God (1 Corinthians 1:30). I had read all those holy books, studied the commentaries, and listened to holy men wax poetic about God, belief, and obedience. All of them pointed to the teachings of the holy teachers of their faith, and how we should follow the inspired wisdom of those men if we wanted to get in good with their gods. But the Bible, unlike any other book I read and studied, makes the claim that we do not just follow the teachings of Jesus; we also worship Jesus as God and Savior.

For that reason, this book has been twenty years in the making. This is the book I wish someone would have written for me, so that at the very least I could know that at the heart of the Christian confession about Jesus, it is not just another religion in a marketplace overrun with religious vendors hawking their beliefs. The Christian confession about Jesus is *the* end of all religion. Jesus is God's answer to our question, "What must I do to be saved?" His answer is: "Nothing. Jesus is the end of all religion." When we come before God to ask, "What must I do to be saved?" his Son holds out his hands and says to us, "It is finished."

Whether you agree or disagree with what I have written, I pray this book inspires you to pray more, read more, meditate on God's Word more, think about your own presuppositions more, and ask yourselves, "What is getting in the way of Christ Jesus being all in all for me?" Maybe it is your preacher, your congregation, or just you. What is preventing God's Word from being your comfort and assurance? Why is your Christian identity not grounded in God's baptismal grace? Why do you not enjoy communing at the Lord's table every week? I hope this book offers an opportunity for you to consider why you are a Christian at all. I hope this book points you to the gospel, gets you excited about it, and drives you to demand it from your preacher, fellow Christians, family, friends, and anyone who wants to make much of their religion at the expense of the good news about Jesus Christ.

The gospel is simple to confess. That is, we are justified by faith alone, through Christ alone, without the works of the Law. And as long as we do not add any limits, measures, or conditions to this, the gospel is easy to confess to others. It is easy for others to confess to us, too! The message that we are justified by faith alone through Christ Jesus is good news anyone can deliver. Anyone can speak the gospel, regardless of social standing, education, or experience. But as simple and easy as the gospel is to announce, we just cannot stop ourselves from wanting to add our two cents to it. We want to confess faith alone out one side of our mouths and then declare out the other side that without works we are not justified. Then we wind ourselves up inventing works we can point at and call "good," so we have something to hang our hat on when our Lord returns on Judgment Day. This is wrong-headed, of course. The good news about Jesus's work for us, his suffering, dying, and rising from death for our justification, is the gospel. It is the only true gospel. The gospel teaches that good works are the fruit of faith, but they are a gift from God and a work of God in us. Faith alone in Christ alone justifies us, because it clings to Jesus alone for everything. Faith talk then is Jesus talk, and so is talk about works. All of faith and works are wrapped in Jesus' faithfulness and work for us.

That is why the gospel is such a simple, comforting message to deliver. Everything has already been done for us by Christ Jesus. Confessing this, God sends us out into the world as his instruments of salvation, with the faith once delivered to all his people—other fruitful workers in the Spirit, just like St. Paul and Titus, and all the saints in every place at every time—to announce the good news that religiosity does not save us. Our beliefs and obedience to God do not save us. Nothing we do and nothing anyone does to us can separate us from the love of God in Jesus Christ. All that is needful for salvation, for us and for the world, has already been accomplished by Jesus.